Critique of Commodity Aesthetics

Critique of Commodity Aesthetics

Appearance, Sexuality and Advertising in Capitalist Society

Wolfgang Fritz Haug
Translated by Robert Bock

University of Minnesota Press, Minneapolis

Published by the University of Minnesota Press 2037 University Avenue
Southeast, Minneapolis MN 55414.
Published simultaneously in Canada by Fitzhenry &
Whiteside Limited, Markham.

Printed in Great Britain.

Library of Congress Cataloguing-in-Publication Data

Haug, Wolfgang Fritz
    Critique of commodity aesthetics.

    Translation of: Kritik der Warenästhetik.
    Bibliography: p.
    Includes index.
    1. Commercial products.   2. Aesthetics.
    3. Fashion and art.   4. Sensuality.   I. Title
    HF1041.H3313   1987   306'.4   86-6917

    ISBN 0-8166-1531-4
    ISBN 0-8166-1532-2 (pbk.)

The University of Minnesota is an equal-opportunity
educator and employer.

Contents

Introduction

Stuart Hall

In the English-speaking world over the last two decades, critical writing in social theory and cultural studies has been overwhelmingly dominated by French writers and theorists. The work of Lévi-Strauss, Barthes, Althusser, Foucault and Derrida has made an indelible and, on the face of it, an unexpected mark on the surface of intellectual life. This is all the more surprising, since the first post-war break into this area in English by Continental thinkers was made in the 1960s, with the extensive publication in English translation, for the first time, of the work of the Frankfurt School and German critical theory, including Adorno, Horkheimer, Marcuse, Habermas and the related writings by Walter Benjamin. In many ways the Frankfurt School set the scene and put in train many of the formative ideas for critical work in the cultural sphere: the essay by Adorno and Horkheimer on 'The Culture Industry' was a seminal instance, in this respect. But, in fact, with the possible exception of Benjamin, the climate of English critical thought has, so far, shown itself relatively inhospitable, in the end, to those influences in anything more than a superficial way.

This turns out on balance to represent a major intellectual loss. There are problems with the way Adorno and Horkheimer advanced their theses about how the modern cultural industries manipulated the needs and instincts of mass society. But this is very different from saying that there is nothing to learn from this attempt to appropriate the theories of Marx and Freud directly into the analysis of modern culture and the mass technologies of modern industrial production – which was at the centre of the project of the Frankfurt School. In more recent times, this absence has meant, for example, that the studies of the mass media in Britain have proceeded largely in ignorance of an extremely interesting and important debate, influenced by the Frankfurt School, about the

impact of commodity production on the sphere of culture, which '
has been raging in German intellectual circles for some time and to
which writers like Hund, Holzer, Dieter Prokop and the work of
Habermas, Oskar Negt and Kluge on the 'public sphere' have made
a major contribution. The vagaries of translation have made this
body of work, together with related studies in the literary field on
'reception aesthetics', virtually invisible in any public way within
recent English debates.

One of the earliest and most important contributions to that
German debate, which put the rich concept of 'commodity
aesthetics' for the first time into the field, is the volume entitled
Critique of Commodity Aesthetics by Wolfgang Fritz Haug, which
finds its long-overdue way into English at last with this Polity
Press/University of Minnesota Press edition.

Haug stands directly within the central preoccupations of the
contributors named above. His work is fed by a number of rich
intellectual streams – German philosophy (which he teaches at the
Free University in Berlin), Marxism, Freud and Brecht, to name
only a few. His whole project, indeed, deserves to be much better
known than it is on this side of the Channel. He was the founder
and, with his wife, Frigga, has remained the principal guide,
mentor and inspirer of a major intellectual/political project centred
around the journal *Das Argument* – an independent critical
Marxist review which first appeared at the same time as the 'New
Left' in Britain. *Das Argument* represented a similar 'break' with
Stalinist and reductionist modes of thought and action on the Left
and – in the forbidding climate of a divided Germany, in the
ideologically polarized context of the European 'front-line' – has
courageously maintained its critical vigour and political independence over several decades. Through it, many of West Germany's
finest young scholars have found their way to a philosophically
informed tradition of independent Marxist thought. *Das Argument*
has been responsible, in recent years, for introducing into German
debates many of the influences and writers which have been making
their own independent mark on ideas in France, Germany and
Italy. It has, for example, gone further than most German circles in
'appropriating' the work of Gramsci into political currency in the
Federal Republic. Its series of books and pamphlets now constitutes one of the richest – and cheapest – sets of 'texts' for critical

students and scholars, across a wide intellectual range. Its *Project Ideologie* has brought together many of the most advanced ideas in the European Left on this troubling question. The journal also constitutes one of the most advanced centres of feminist scholarship and research in Europe.

Critique of Commodity Aesthetics does not represent Wolf Haug's most recent thinking on the subject. But this revised edition – the eighth – with a special Introduction by the author, makes available for the first time a 'classic' set of arguments. The book is addressed to the central issue which Adorno and Horkheimer first put on the intellectual agenda: the question of the relationship between modern forms of commodity production under advanced capitalism, the structure of human needs and what Haug calls 'the fate of sensuality'. Haug roots his discourse in Marx's analysis of the commodity form in *Capital* and the discussion of 'needs' in the *Economic and Philosophical Manuscripts*. Moving, in a vigorous and supple discourse, between high philosophical theory and the mundane world of modern advertising and design, he exploits and develops the contradiction between 'use'- and 'exchange'-value, in the context of modern cultural and social life. In ways which few comparable English texts could match, he shows how the development of modern commodity forms, dominated by exchange-value, intersects directly with the realm of human needs and the domain of sensuality. The implied 'project' of the book is to undermine that barrier between 'outside' and 'inside' – between social production and human psychology – which, it often seems, is erected for us not only by the tendencies of a whole intellectual culture but by the very English language itself. He spans the divide which has proved such an awkward stumbling block in this field of scholarly research – that between the incorporation into commodity forms of modern aesthetics, on the one hand, and the analysis of political economy, on the other.

This is the volume which opened up the whole argument around 'commodity aesthetics'. But the most significant result of Haug's work – and the point which most clearly represents his 'break' with and advance on the classic formulations of the Frankfurt School – lies in the area of his discussion of 'manipulation'. It was the thesis concerning the powers of the modern cultural industries in the area of mass manipulation, advanced by the Frankfurt

School under the rubric of the 'eclipse of enlightenment', which constituted, at one and the same time, the force of the critique they advanced, and the difficulties their work presented. Marcuse raised this philosophical critique to its highest political point of intervention in the 1960s with the theory of 'one dimensional society' and, in *Eros and Civilization* and other writings, he addressed the same nexus between production, culture and 'needs'. But the theory, despite its philosophical sophistication, appeared, at once, both startling, in many ways terrifying but also, too one-sided.

Haug does not refuse the thesis of 'manipulation'. But he does advance the argument considerably by showing the two-sided, contradictory nature of the manipulative process. He accomplishes this by what he calls a 'critique' of manipulation – that is, by exploring the conditions within which manipulation can occur, once we have ditched the simplified solaces of conspiracy theory. As he puts the argument in his Introduction, 'manipulation could only be effective if it "somehow" latched on to the "objective interests" of those being manipulated . . . while pursuing their interests.' Even manipulative phenomena must 'speak the language of real needs' – they must express real needs, even in an alienated or estranged mode, if they are to inscribe themselves in the domain of 'subjective sensuality' (the *cognito sensitiva*) where needs are 'experienced'.

The book traces, in a series of probing investigations, the various dimensions along which modern commodity production, as it increasingly incorporates the aesthetic dimension (in, for example, advertising or contemporary design) develops a discourse which connects with and transforms 'the sensual awareness' of modern consumer society. In so doing, it plays, with increasing complexity, across the ambiguities of the 'real' and the 'fantastic'. The whole argument is sustained by a self-reflexive philosophical discourse which doubles on itself, lifting the book into an altogether different domain from that occupied by most available 'analyses' of, say, contemporary advertising or design trends.

Haug's argument is certainly not completed in this volume. It bears, as he himself says, the provisional sign: 'Further work needed here.' But it is a bold and challenging start in what, for the English debates, is virtually a new direction –uncharted waters. It is sincerely to be hoped that it will have the major impact it deserves on critical work and scholarship in this area.

Author's Introduction

The *Critique of Commodity Aesthetics* is a contribution to the social analysis of the fate of sensuality and the development of needs within capitalism. It is a critique in so far as it represents the mode of functioning of its object domain alongside its conditions of possible existence, its contradictory character and its historical development. The intention is not to offer yet another condemnation of advertising manipulation and the like. The tendency of such literature is to draw conclusions by analogy from surface phenomena regarding the supposed basic character of society. Such theories remain in part caught up in surface appearances, which they use to make into absolute assertions about the nature of society; and in part they set up immediate relationships between each isolated phenomenon and a speculatively derived whole. This sort of approach cannot differentiate between the unintended effects of certain processes and the almost conspiratorial effects deliberately produced by a hidden subject.

We do not have to go far to find examples of such dubious theory. It is perhaps worth mentioning in this context my own essay 'Zur Ästhetik von Manipulation' ['On the Aesthetics of Manipulation'], in which these mistakes are apparent.[1] In writing that essay – and I was following famous examples – I gave the impression that I knew absolutely everything about 'the whole'. Accordingly, I approached the individual phenomena by interpreting their features immediately in terms of a theory of 'the whole'. Nevertheless, this first essay – in which incidentally the term 'commodity aesthetics' was coined – contains an insight into a problem unresolved by critical theory, a school of thought which had initially impressed me greatly. In line with this insight a critique of manipulation should explore the conditions within which manipulation can operate, if only to be able to counteract it.

However, manipulation could only be effective if it 'somehow' latched on to the 'objective interests' of those being manipulated. 'The masses,' I maintained, 'are being manipulated while pursuing their interests. Manipulative phenomena, therefore, still speak the language of real needs even if it is as it were an alien expression of those needs which are now estranged and distorted beyond recognition.' I summed up this premise, which contained a programme for research and a political perspective *in nuce,* in one sentence: 'The objective realities of happiness and unhappiness form the basis of manipulation.'[2] Only a critique which adheres to these moments in its object of criticism can become a determined negation, determined in the sense that it knows what it is aiming at and thus with whom it is allied.

Theorizing 'from the standpoint of resulting phenomena' (Marx) encounters a wealth of empirical phenomena, which may often seem very interesting, but which remains more or less at the mercy of the object domain in its formative concept. 'It is, in reality,' Marx comments on the methodology of a critique of religion, 'much easier to discover by analysis the earthly kernel of the misty creations of religion than to do the opposite, i.e. to develop from the actual, given relations of life the forms in which these have been apotheosized. The latter method is the only materialist, and therefore the only scientific one.'[3] The following work applies this method of unfolding the phenomena under investigation from their fundamental economic relations. At the same time it necessarily proceeds from the elementary unit to complex combinations. Our method begins, therefore, with the derivation of its concepts in an analysis of simple exchange. We shall trace the evolution of the functions and interests inherent in exchange relations, up to the emergence of monopoly capitalism. We conclude by considering, in a related field, how this aesthetics is used for the legitimization of state power, as illustrated by the example of fascism as a type of pseudo-socialism. The investigation thus proceeds along several strata in a development from what might be termed base to superstructure.

Although Marx had only acknowledged the relations being studied here in passing, and never analysed them himself – if one overlooks some flashes of insight in his 'Economic and Philosophical Manuscripts' – the concepts and functional analysis on which this book builds were nevertheless already formulated in *Capital*. The task is not simply one of describing, classifying or interpreting the empirical phenomena, but of deriving them from their economic basis. But this presents the same consequence in the field of commodity aesthetics, as that of which Engels warned *Capital*'s English readers: 'There is, however, one difficulty we could not spare the reader: the use of certain terms in a sense different from what they have, not only in common life, but in ordinary political economy.' Bourgeois economic theory 'has generally been content to take, just as they were, the terms of commercial and industrial life, and to operate with them, entirely failing to see that by so doing it confined itself within the narrow circle of ideas expressed by those terms.'[4] The derivation of these phenomena and the reconstruction of their development demand a language different from their own.

Inevitably in the present context a number of new terms were coined in order to define the sensual phenomena in their specific economic form and function. These terms, such as 'aesthetic abstraction', 'technocracy of sensuality', 'aesthetic promise of use-value' and 'aesthetic innovation', are defined in the course of this investigation. This terminology, which was introduced in two essays of mine (1969/70),[5] has now passed the test as an analytical tool, as it has since been usefully employed in several studies and discussions. The most comprehensive concept to be introduced is that of 'commodity aesthetics' itself. It designates a complex which springs from the commodity form of the products and which is functionally determined by exchange-value – a complex of material phenomena and of the sensual subject–object relations conditioned by these phenomena. The analysis of these relations reveals the subjective element in the political economy of capitalism in so far as subjectivity is at once a result and a prerequisite of its functioning. In as much as these phenomena are derived from the basic functional system of commodity production, this critique differs not only from theories that immediately wish to interpret 'the whole' starting from every individual phenomenon, but also from those that consider separate phenomena in isolation – and usually without derivation – taken from the complex of commodity aesthetics, e.g. advertising and design. Under this methodology not even the selected phenomena can be adequately comprehended.

The concept of 'aesthetics' is used here in a way that will confuse readers who associate it exclusively with art. Firstly, it is employed in the sense in which it originally appeared in the language of scholars, as *cognito sensitiva,* a term used to designate sensual understanding. Beyond that, it is used as ambiguously as the context requires, sometimes stressing subjective sensuality, sometimes the role of the sensual object. The term 'commodity aesthetics', specifically, narrows it down in two respects: on the one hand to 'beauty', i.e. an appearance which appeals to the senses; and, on the other hand, to a beauty developed in the service of the realization of exchange-value, whereby commodities are designed to stimulate in the onlooker the desire to possess and the impulse to buy. In so far as that which is beautiful about a commodity appeals to people, it engages their sensual understanding and the sensual interest which in turn determines it. The transformation of the world of useful objects into commodities triggers instinctual responses, and the functional means by which not only the world of sensual objects but also human sensuality itself is remoulded again and again. 'The moulding of sensuality', therefore, is another term used to articulate questions central to this investigation.

I received encouragement to explore this dimension from Norbert Elias, who investigates the evolutionary stages of 'affect moulding' in the Western bourgeoisie in his theory of the civilizing process.[6] However, where Elias derives the mechanics of the process he describes from a formalization of its phenomenal traits, the critique of commodity aesthetics offers an insight into the concrete economic functional circuits involved, which help to explain with more precision certain processes of affect moulding.

The task I set myself, therefore, was to derive the phenomena of commodity aesthetics from their economic basis and to develop and present them within their systematic connections. This could not be achieved by way of empirical analysis. Empirical material is only introduced occasionally, as in a spot-check for exemplary analysis. This procedure has the inevitable disadvantage, it seems to me, of inaccurately shifting the emphasis, if the reader does not constantly keep in mind the limited scope of these illustrations. At each stage of the development, the reader will be able to think up further, perhaps better, examples. For our subject matter is without doubt striking; it goes beyond any fantasy, yet its clarity can outdo any didactic intention of plain-speaking. But precisely therein lies the danger. If approached without due care, and without a well-constructed theory and system of concepts, the material, while seeming obvious, often points us in the wrong direction. It *is* fantastic, but if one allows oneself to be fascinated by it, we will end up producing absurd theories.

The reader is therefore advised to pay particular attention to the development of the concepts. They are offered as tools and are meant to enable the user to understand each phenomenon as it is determined by economic forms and functions and to describe its origin and function respecting different modes of causality and effect.

The field of commodity aesthetics, whose systematic exploration began with this book, merits more detailed study, because of its indisputable significance in underpinning the power relations of late capitalism. For this reason, this book may conclude in the same way as Horkheimer and Adorno's chapter on 'The Culture Industry' in *Dialectic of Enlightenment*, with the lapidary phrase 'To be continued . . .'[7] But if critical theory has not proved suitable for continuation in the sense that, because of its underived and analogical-hermeneutic concepts, it has only ever managed to paraphrase itself endlessly, then this study may be put to the same test.

Berlin, 1971

Postscript to the Eighth German Edition

Commodity aesthetics is one of the most powerful forces in capitalist society. It counters the traditional ideological powers – notably religion, education and art – and infiltrates them to a certain extent. In conjunction with the new media, it is probably the dominant force in the collective imagination of millions of people every day. This subject is thus certainly not just the current fashion. Even when I made a conscious decision to turn away from it, believing I had finished with the subject, I remained in its grasp.

Perhaps our approach will be facilitated by glancing over the development of my methodological conception of commodity aesthetics. It can be said that I have presented this subject matter three times – four, if we count the *Zeitungsroman*[1] – but each presentation is moulded according to its own critical and theoretical paradigm. As I wrote in the Foreword to the first (1971) edition of this book, my orientation in the sixties was primarily towards models from critical theory and the work of Freud. At the beginning of the seventies, motivated back into action by the student movement, I worked out the theory of commodity aesthetics, as this book demonstrates, as an extension of Marx's 'Critique of Political Economy'. A criticism of the edition of 1971 would be that it is restricted by the model of a derivative Marxism, which was particularly influential on the left at that time. At least, the presentation is not sufficiently delineated to guard against stances which take no account of human activity. Moreover, the way the work is constructed suggests a progression from the economic to the political and ideological, as if the latter were simply an expression of economic categories from which they could directly be derived. In short, that edition is not free from economistic distortions.

Such economism can at first be seen in the tacit suggestion that certain everyday phenomena are purely economically determined. Put another way, the economistic illusion consists, among other things, in the unquestioning acceptance that the abstractions of the critique of economy can immediately grasp empirical phenomena. In short, economism proceeds with an empiricist misunderstanding of abstractions. However, let us not throw the baby out with the bath-water! To criticize the absolutization of economism and its empiricist misunderstanding of abstractions should not be understood as a refusal of abstraction and a rejection of the 'Critique of Political Economy'. Without abstractions there can be no articulated analysis, and without a critique of political economy we cannot conceptualize the society we live in. Taking human activity adequately into consideration in this theory cannot mean leaving untouched the economic forms, needs and relations in which people act. It would be particularly absurd in the case of commodity aesthetics to ignore the fact that its current dominant form is the aesthetics of the monopoly-commodity, i.e. the form in which transnational enterprises in particular intervene directly in the collective imaginations of cultures. Of course, the critique of economy must be able to recognize its limitations even in this area. The categories of the critique of economy alone cannot ascertain *how* commodity aesthetics intervenes in the collective imagination, how it reacts with the traditional institutions, and above all how all this is translated into everyday life. Concrete phenomena cannot be deduced: they must be reproduced in thought through the methodological synthesis of many abstract determinants. And we cannot renounce with impunity this insight from Marx – that one-time Young Hegelian who later surpassed his mentor. Finally, we must take account of the interference relation of praxis. Marxist theory often seems to oscillate between instructions on how to change these relations and the derivation of their development on the basis of objective laws, over whose operation human actions have no influence. The second viewpoint in this puzzle was not Marx's and especially not the opinion of the later Marx, although it was widespread among Marxists. While a critical analysis of the relations and of the possibilities for action are taken up by a social movement from which action does result, already these relations are no longer exactly the same. The concepts must be formed in such a way as to make praxis possible, while not becoming obsolete themselves in the process. As Brecht emphasized time and again, a theory may not be *too* comprehensive nor *too* complete. It can clarify struggles but not anticipate their outcome, and it is as this sort of open-ended theory that it can contribute to the capacity for action.

In the seventies I developed, on the one hand, a new reading of the 'Critique of Political Economy',[2] which because of its interpretation of economic forms as *forms of praxis* was compatible with the demand for orientation towards action. On the other hand I turned my attention to investigating anew questions of ideology and culture. Step by step I developed a new approach to cultural as well as ideological concepts, to representations of inter- (or counter-) action in cultural activity from below and to ideological power from above, and last but not least to commodity aesthetics.[3] Eventually I constructed the theory of commodity aesthetics for a third – and I assumed last – time with particular regard to the problems outlined above. Above all it had to be compatible with the new theory of culture and ideology. These three theoretical areas had to be integrated into a theoretical framework of capitalist mass-culture. This task is hopefully approaching a speedy conclusion.[4]

The reader should take heed of the suggestions outlined above, namely avoiding an empiricist short circuit; avoiding economistic absolutization; remembering the need to take human actions into account and therefore to suppress the illusions based on the logic of derivation – which is a nightmare. If these suggestions are taken up then this text will retain its own value beyond its documentary character, in particular because the material from the everyday economic life of our society has hardly been incorporated anywhere else.

Berlin, June 1983

Chapter One

1 The origin of commodity aesthetics in the contradiction of the exchange relation

If we ask what conditions must be fulfilled within the framework of an exchange relation in order that two owners may exchange commodities, we immediately encounter a practical difficulty, from whose resolution the ever-increasing form, money, develops. In the first place, the self-evident condition which renders an exchange meaningful contains a problem which hinders the transaction as well as the extension of exchange relations: only the exchange of qualitatively different things is meaningful. The respective owners must be able to spare them, i.e. they must have no need or use for them; the non-owning party, by contrast, must need them in order to be interested in acquiring them by exchange. Only in the event of two such complementary relationships is exchange possible and thus mutually meaningful. In short, non-owning need on the one side must coincide with not-needing ownership on the other. If those who have what I need do not need what I have, then they will not be interested in an exchange.

Secondly there must be an equivalence and the possibility of expressing it, without which trade cannot take place. Thus it must be possible to say of two things that they have equal value. But how is this equivalence to be expressed when each commodity can only ever prove its value as an exchange-value? This means that its value only appears at first as an amount of another commodity which can be exchanged for it. Outside of an exchange relationship, each commodity cannot express itself on the question of its value, while within a relationship with another commodity the exchange relation must be found for every type and quality of commodity separately. The resolution, from which money will develop, is approached when, in the search for the value of two commodities, the exchange relations already known for each commodity are expressed in terms of a third commodity. This third element now acts as a means of expressing the value of the commodities to be exchanged: the relationship to this third commodity forms the basis of the language of value, in which the goods to be exchanged can express their equivalence.

Money, as the generalized and further developed form of this 'third commodity', serves a dual purpose. On the one hand, it functions as an expression of value, thus making different things comparable and measurable. Money serves as a uniform material for the language of valuation. On the other hand, since the exchange-value of each commodity has an independent monetary form, money separates the too-complex process of commodity exchange into two acts 'by splitting up the direct identity present in this case between the exchange of one's own product and the acquisition of someone else's into the two antithetical segments of sale and purchase.'[1] No longer is it an immediate exchange of one particular commodity for another of an equally specific kind. At first a certain amount of this 'general commodity' or 'money commodity', which represents the independent form of the general exchange-value for all other commodities, is appropriated by exchange. It is only through a second act of exchange, externally independent from the first and possibly distant in time and space, that the exchange value in its independent form as 'money', this 'abstract form of the general wealth', is then exchanged for the commodity required. In the form of money, the third factor of comparison (*tertium comparationis*) can stand up for itself, step between all the commodities, and negotiate their exchange.

Thus, an abstraction is accomplished: while the exchange-value has detached itself from any specific commodity-body, it has become independent of any specific need. Whoever possesses this is invested with power over all manner of qualities, limited only by the quantity at his or her disposal.

Money facilitates, expedites and generalizes exchange. As a solution to the difficulties of simple and unmediated exchange, it also heightens a contradiction already inherent therein. The driving force and determining aim for each side involved in a two-sided commodity exchange is the need for the other's use-value. At the same time one's own commodity along with the other's needs serve only as a means to this particular end. The goal of each party is but the other's means to reach their own goal by way of the exchange. Thus in a single exchange, two-times-two antagonistic positions oppose one another. Each party takes up a standpoint of exchange-value as well as of a fixed use-value, and each use-value standpoint is opposed by an exchange-value standpoint, from which it may be defrauded.

Whoever assumes this use-value standpoint, his or her own personal integrity is at stake to the extent that, as a sensual being, one is directed to the use-value; from the point of view of exchange-value, the use-value is only the bait. So long as both positions are maintained undifferentiated by both parties involved in the exchange, the contradiction of interests remains bound up in the equality of both positions.

When money intervenes, the relationship is changed. Money as the mediator not only splits the exchange into two acts, into buying and selling, but it isolates the opposing standpoints. The buyer is concerned with the satisfaction of needs, thus aiming to achieve a certain use-value, by means of exchange-value in the form of money. For the seller, the same use-value is merely a means to convert the exchange-value of his or her commodities into money; in other words, to extract the exchange-value from the commodities and make it independent as money. From the point of view of exchange-value, each commodity, regardless of its particular form, matters only as an exchange-value which still needs to be realized as money: its form as use-value is merely a transitory phase and a prison. From the point of view of needing the use-value, the object of the exercise has been achieved if the purchased article is usable and satisfactory; from the exchange-value side this is achieved when the exchange-value is converted into monetary form.

In so far as the logic of exchange is the determinant, the seller values the material and immaterial things which the other person needs to survive – his or her necessities of life – practically, the other person's life functions as a mere instrument in obtaining exchange-value. While one values the commodity as a means of survival, the other sees such necessities as a means of valorization. The difference between these positions is very striking; but as soon as they begin to exist separately, the contradiction becomes formidable. This contradiction becomes a deciding factor in the production of commodities, and equally in their development and methods of manufacture. In the divergence between need and buying power it becomes a major consideration for an increasingly wide sector of the population. As purchasing power lags behind production capacity, this contradiction periodically affects capital in terms of crises, and threatens to withdraw from the working classes the possibility of wage-labour and thus their material livelihood.

Within the context of this investigation, we do not propose to discuss the way this contradiction is exacerbated into a crisis, nor bourgeois attempts to control it. Instead, let us look at the illusory solution [*Scheinlösung*] to this fundamental contradiction which, from its historical beginnings, has been typical for the normal, current functioning of a social system based upon private enterprise and the division of labour.

Commodity production has as its aim not the creation of certain use-values, as such, but rather manufacture for sale. Use-value only figures in the calculations of the commodity producer in terms of buyer-expectation which must be taken into consideration. Not only are the ends and means for buyer and seller in opposition, but the same act also takes place at different times and with different meanings for each party. As far as the exchange-value is concerned, the transaction is completed and the purpose realized with the sale itself. From the point of view of use-value and need, the sale is only the start, and is the prerequisite to the buyer's realization of purpose in the use and enjoyment of the purchase.

From out of the contradiction of use-value and exchange-value, thus distributed between individuals, there appears a tendency time and again to modify the commodity-body, i.e. its use-form. Henceforth in all commodity production a double reality is produced: first the use-value; second, and more importantly, the *appearance* of use-value. For, until the sale is completed (and the exchange-value has been realized), use-value figures only in as much as the buyer promises him- or herself the use-value of the commodity. From the seller's (i.e. the exchange-value) position, until the sale is effected, the commodity's promise of use-value is all that counts. Right from the start, therefore, because of its economic function, the emphasis is on what the use-value *appears* to be – which, in terms of a single sales-act, is liable to be no more than mere illusion. The aesthetics of the commodity in its widest meaning – the sensual appearance and the conception of its use-value – become detached from the object itself. Appearance becomes just as important – and practically more so – than the commodity's being itself. Something that is simply useful but does not appear to be so, will not sell, while something that seems to be useful, will sell. Within the system of selling and buying, the aesthetic illusion – the commodity's promise of use-value – enters the arena as an independent function in selling. For economic reasons it is only natural and, under the pressures of competition, ultimately necessary to gain technological control over and independent production of this aesthetic process.

The commodity's aesthetic promise of use-value thus becomes an instrument in accumulating money. Its opposite (i.e. exchange-value) interest elicits from the standpoint of exchange-value an exaggeration of the apparent use-value of the commodity, the more so because use-value is of secondary importance from the standpoint of exchange-value. Sensuality in this context becomes the vehicle of an economic function, the subject and object of an economically functional fascination. Whoever controls the product's appearance can control the fascinated public by appealing to them sensually.

This means that even in the pre-history of capitalism, in the relation of interests in exchange, the tendency towards a 'technocracy of sensuality' was pre-shaped economically in the subordination of use-value to exchange-value. Since, within a developed system of private commodity production, it is essentially exchange-value which is produced rather than the social livelihood and the means to satisfy needs; and since commodity characteristics, which solicit the needs of potential customers, only serve as a device for obtaining their exchange-value, the young Marx's analysis in his 'Economic and Philosophical Manuscripts' is valid here: every product of private commodity production 'is a bait with which to entice the essence of the other, his money', which is all that counts from the position of exchange-value. On the other hand, 'every real or potential need' of the sensuous human being is 'a weakness which will tempt the fly onto the limetwig.' Wherever there is a want, a need, a demand, there is a producer who offers his 'labour of love' with the most 'glittering illusion' – and presents the bill.[2] Just because it is completely inessential from the standpoint of exchange-value, the sensuous being of those with money is preyed upon, sustained and attended to in all its fancies, moods and whims, as the industrial capitalist caters for 'his neighbour's most depraved fancies, panders to his needs, excites unhealthy appetites in him and pounces on every weakness.'[3]

2   Powerful stimuli as an instrument of merchant–capitalist valorization

Before exploring specific aesthetic stimuli we must define further the standpoint of exchange-value. As soon as the exchange-value has become independent in the form of money, the whole exchange-value standpoint is provided with the precondition for its independence too. In the form of money, exchange-value is no longer attached to any sensuous need and is stripped of any complex sensuous quality.

While it is meaningless to accumulate certain sensual use-values indefinitely, since their worth is limited by their usefulness, the accretion of exchange-value, being merely quantitative, suffers no such constraints. With money, originally the objectification of a function of exchange, comes a force of unknown quality in the world – abstract wealth or independent exchange-value. It initiates an interest alongside this independence, namely valorization. Money-lending and trade are its first major historical manifestations, and in this chapter we will examine some characteristics of merchant capital whose heyday in Europe coincided with that of early capitalism.

The business of merchant capital is to buy in order to sell at a profit. Its activity was initially transregional, if not transcultural, and its strength lay historically in foreign trade. Novelty and distinctiveness were the keys that opened up markets for capitalist trade.[4] In order to invade local markets or expand into regions previously unfamiliar with commodity production, merchant capital requires specific categories of commodity. Three groups of commodity have aroused quite a furore and have paved the way for a global change in trade relations; firstly military supplies, secondly textiles and thirdly stimuli and luxury goods. Just as firearms and 'fire-water' invaded the New World, so powerful stimulants have entered European history as instruments of merchant–capitalist val-orization. The European powers which rose to world domination by this means were, in order of appearance, Venice, the Netherlands and England.

3   Courtship, luxury of the aristocracy and clear-headed
     bourgeois intoxication; chocolate, tea, tobacco, coffee

When Marx says 'commodities are in love with money' and that they ogle it with their price 'casting wooing glances',[5] the metaphor is operating on a socio-historical basis, for one category of power-ful stimuli in the production of commodities for valorization is that of erotic attraction. Thus a whole range of commodities can be seen casting flirtatious glances at the buyers, in an exact imitation of or even surpassing the buyers' own glances, which they use in courting their human objects of affection. Whoever goes courting makes themselves attractive and desirable. All manner of jewellery, fabrics, scents and colours offer themselves as means of presenting beauty and desirability. Thus, commodities borrow their aes-thetic language from human courtship; but then the relationship is reversed and people borrow their aesthetic expression from the world of the commodity. This indicates an initial feedback from the stimulating use-form of commodities, which is itself provoked by valorization motives, to human sensuality. Not only does this alter the possibilities of expressing the human instinctual structure, but the whole emphasis changes: powerful aesthetic stimulation, exchange-value and libido cling to one another like the folk in the tale of the Golden Goose – the means of expression undergo rises in value – and they cost a fortune.

It is thus that the bourgeoisie provides the aristocrat with a 'wider range of opportunities for the other's self-indulgence and flatters him through his products – for his products are so many base compliments to the appetites of the spendthrift – but also manages to appropriate for himself . . . the other's dwindling power.[6]

Soon the rising bourgeoisie lent money to the aristocrat at extor-tionate rates of interest so that he could buy his ostentatious and luxurious commodities until, piece by piece, the noble's lands and property fell into the hands of the bourgeoisie. They capitalized on this to the cost of all unproductive consumers, who were driven to begging or to the workhouse until the rise of capitalist production recognized their use as cheap wage-labour.

Luxury commodities with their powerful sensual stimuli made a significant contribution to the redistribution of wealth, through a revolution in its valorization, that is, original accumulation. This process is based, functionally and historically, in the foundations of bourgeois society and is completely characteristic of it. 'Each person,' Marx wrote in his 'Economic and Philosophical Manuscripts', 'speculates on creating a new need in the other, with the aim of forcing him to make a new sacrifice, placing him in a new dependence and seducing him into a new kind of enjoyment and hence into economic ruin.'[7] And the bourgeoisie have learnt this lesson well. Idleness and luxury, from which they derive a profit, are frowned on among themselves, and are even more despised among the lower classes. The enjoyment of the early capitalists 'is only incidental, a means of relaxation; it is subordinated to production, it is a calculated and even an economical form of pleasure.' In the persona of the capitalists, in so far as they are an embodiment of capital, 'enjoyment is . . . subsumed under capital, and the pleasure-seeking individual under the capitalizing individual.'[8]

If only to guard against uncontrolled libidinal outbreaks that might threaten their adjustment to office life, the capitalists compensate with pleasures highly suited to their bourgeois activities: tobacco, coffee, but most of all tea, for which there was a tremendous demand in the seventeenth century, while the clergy and aristocracy continued to consume chocolate and sugar. Since chocolate was a commodity of Catholic colonialist extraction, warnings against tea and tobacco, the Devil's playthings, were preached from the pulpit, while cocoa was commended as a remedy for plague and cholera.

Bourgeois art celebrated both coffee and tea in cantatas, songs and poems:

> Often, however, it was the East India Company on whose behalf and at whose cost these panegyrics were commissioned in order to increase turnover. Tea was declared a 'divine plant', to be compared with nectar, and a daily 40 to 50 cups of it was recommended. A

Dutch doctor living in Hamburg, who prescribed large quantities of tea to wean his patients off spirits, was suspected of having been bribed by the tea merchants.[9]

This doctor's intervention 'in the interests of a suffering populace and the Dutch merchants', by administering this expensive but mild intoxicant to cure alcoholism, was an action symptomatic of his class.

In 1718 a Paris physician declared to his faculty that coffee was an effective drug for the treatment of drunkenness after the consumption of alcohol. Merchants had brought coffee to Europe from Constantinople, where the 'Turkish drink' was served as a substitute for proscribed alcohol. For, even when intoxicated, the businessman needed a clear head. The first coffee-house opened in London in 1652, and fifty years later, according to Zetzner, there were 1,000 such establishments, which also offered pipes of tobacco.[10]

At about the same time, Mandeville remarked on the great impact commodities of mass luxury such as coffee, tea, tobacco and purple cloth were having on the national economy. The desire to imitate, he wrote, had the effect that children and young people 'accustom themselves by degrees to the use of things that were irksome, if not intolerable to them at first; till they know not how to leave them, and are often very sorry for having inconsiderately increased the necessaries of life without any necessity. What estates have been got by tea and coffee!'

Consider also, Dr Mandeville continues, in order to pre-empt any moral objections, 'what a vast traffic is done' and 'what a variety of labour is performed in the world to the maintenance of thousands of families that altogether depend on two silly if not odious customs; the taking of snuff and smoking of tobacco; both which it is certain do infinitely more hurt than good to those that are addicted to them!'[11] Perhaps it is not irrelevant here to hint that the creation and control of a need for luxury is in no way a phenomenon restricted to late capitalism, as so many theorists, notably of the late-1960s' student movement, believed.

4   Capitalist mass-production and the problem of profit
     realization – the aesthetics of the mass-produced
     commodity

The capitalization of commodity production unleashes a powerful
incentive for the development of techniques for the manufacture of
relative surplus-value, i.e. to increase profits by increasing productivity, particularly through the use of machinery and the establishment of large industries. At the same time the tendency is to draw
all members of society into distributing commodities through the
market. Hence with the spread of mass demand, both technology
and the productive forces of mass manufacture are promoted.
From now on it is no longer primarily expensive luxury commodities that determine big business but the relatively cheap mass-
produced articles. Realization, size and rate of profit are now
determined by the valorization functions typical of industrial
capital.

   Within the production sphere the following functions of investment return are of interest in this context. First, the reduction
of working hours per item through an increased productivity
of labour, which includes the trend towards eliminating manual
work (which will return as a valuable component in the advertising
of certain luxury goods) and the development of technology in
mass-producing standardized articles. Second, the lowering of
the sections of constant capital which go into raw materials and
other components. Third, the shortening of production time such
as reducing, by artificial means, the storage time needed for
maturation.

   It is obvious that all these changes must modify the appearance
of the end product. However, just as many means appear for cover-
ing up or compensating for these modifications by the additional
production of the commodity's appearance. Sophisticated treatment of surfaces or colouring can disguise a deterioration in the
material or the craftsmanship. Brandy, instead of deriving its
brownish colour from maturing in oak casks for years, is tinted
with caramel to maintain its appearance. Or, as well as shortening
the maturation process, essential ingredients can be omitted, and
the limits of commodity faking are exceeded. As Engels illustrated

in the case of wine and rum, this tendency increased especially with the rise of distillation from potatoes on a large industrial scale by Prussian estate owners, which drove petit-bourgeois distilleries out of business; 'The means of getting drunk, which used to cost three or four times as much, was now available everyday even to the poorest.'[12] Prussian brandy, incidentally, contributed greatly to the brutalization and the dulling of senses among the working class, owing to its high content of fusel oil.

In the sphere of circulation we are concerned with only one matter: a change of form has to occur here, value and surplus-value have to be realized. Already the slightest delay could lead to ruin. The factor awaiting the realization of its exchange-value is no longer just the commodity but commodity-capital. The unrelenting threat of ruin, combined with the irresistible attractiveness emanating from the forward thrust of the profit motive, turns the waiting for realization into a feverish activity. Every hold-up in circulation incurs costs and reduces the commodity value. And the capitalist, under pressure of competition, cannot compensate for these losses with a price increase.

> The eventual purchaser would laugh at the capitalist if he said: 'I could not sell my commodity for six months, and it not only cost me so and so much in idle capital to maintain if for these six months, but also caused expenses . . .' 'So much the worse for you,' the buyer will say, 'for next to you there is another seller whose commodity was finished only yesterday. Your commodity is evidently a white elephant, and probably more or less damaged by the ravages of time. You must therefore sell cheaper than your rival.'[13]

The threat of becoming a white elephant is a constant headache for commodity capital, personified by the capitalist. For the existence of old stock spells economic death for any capital trapped in commodity form. Marx uses the strongest terms to describe this problem of profit realization. Here the commodity has to perform its *salto mortale,* the death-defying leap, which carries the risk that it might break its neck.[14] Here the exchange-value, trapped in the body of a commodity, yearns to be rescued and released into monetary form. It all revolves around – as it is called in *Capital* – 'the miracle of this transsubstantiation'.[15] This is the moment when and the place where the merchandise casts its loving glances.

'If the soul of the commodity,' Walter Benjamin writes in *Charles Baudelaire. A lyric poet in the era of high capitalism*, 'which Marx occasionally mentions in jest existed, it would be the most empathetic ever encountered in the realm of souls, for it would have to see in everyone the buyer in whose hand and house it wants to nestle.'[16] The valorization function seeking an answer to the problem of realization, expresses itself precisely in the exaggerated appearance of use-value, and thus the exchange-value lurking in the commodity rushes towards the money. The lust for money is the reason why, under capitalist production, the commodity is created in the image of the consumer's desires. Later on this image, divorced from its commodity, is the subject of advertising promotion.

5   The first effect and instrument of monopolization:
aesthetic monopolization of use-value ('brand')
– bordering on the faking of commodities; the fight for
and with names – Rosy vs Rosy-Rosy; competition of
images; Helmut Schmidt's conception of political
confrontation as a competition of mere impressions;
Goebbels as a 'technician of trademarks'

The empathy of the commodities with the buyer's soul, which Benjamin describes, comes up against the very limits of the market. So long as several manufacturers competed within a certain range of commodities, commodity aesthetics remained bound up with the commodity-body itself. Simultaneously, it was determined by a certain standard of use-value through relatively similar production methods. So long as commodity aesthetics represented nothing more than the embodiment of this use-value in a certain category of commodities, its specific origin faded into insignificance. However, since this insignificance is only a means to an end, the relationship already contains its potential reversal within itself. It will be the function of the particular, of novelty and originality, to effect this reversal. The fact that the production of use-values is only a means to valorization has the effect that private capital attempts to raise itself above use-value.

'This is a golden age in trademarks,' reads a text from 1905 quoted by Baran and Sweezy, a time when almost any maker of a worthy product can lay down the lines of a demand that will not only grow with years beyond anything that has ever been known before, but it will become to some degree a monopoly. . . . Everywhere . . . there are opportunities to take the lead in advertising – to replace dozens of mongrel, unknown, unacknowledged makes of a fabric, a dress essential, a food with a standard trade-marked brand, backed by the national advertising that in itself has come to be guarantee of worth with the public.[17]

Together with these 'dozens of mongrel, unknown makes' of nameless everyday products, it was always the generally accepted use-value which was discarded as an obstacle to valorization. With the subordination and control of certain use-values by private enterprise, commodity aesthetics receives not only a qualitatively new meaning – to codify a new class of information – but it also detaches itself from the body of the commodity, whose styling is heightened by the packaging and widely distributed by advertising.

The means of establishing this monopolistic situation is to elevate the commodity to the status of brand-name. All available aesthetic devices are employed to further this end. The decisive factor, however, is the concentration into one named character of all the aesthetic, visual and verbal communications contained in the styling of the commodity. The common language used for this purpose at most serves to name the manufacturers and to give them an air of prestige. While brand-named goods which are distributed locally seem laughable, like other local customs, names and dialects, the trans-regional brand-names of large companies impose themselves on to the public's experience and virtually assume the status of natural phenomena.[18]

The companies and their advertising agencies deliberately aim at this target. 'Forget the word "banana!" Remember Chiquita!' was the advert of the United Fruit Company in Germany.[19] In present-day capitalist society, there are types of commodities, whose generic concepts expressing their use-values are no longer made available to people. Their place has been taken by a copyright trademark, and it is perhaps only in the instructions for use or list of ingredients (only printed when required by law) that there might remain a trace of the now eliminated concepts of use-value. This is a major reason for the radical decline in the practical knowledge of commodities among the inhabitants of monopoly capitalist societies. The monopolies often monopolize even the most basic technical and chemical knowledge through the use of brand-names. What every housewife knew in the old days is now shrouded in secrecy and we become more dependent on the brand-named products. 'Simply take *XYZ*!'

The sign of quality under which an article is promoted is primarily determined, economically, by the motivation of targeted consumer groups and the requirements of large-scale marketing. The sign, and the direct and mediated promise of use-value with which it is equipped, must be completely dissociated from the specific constitution of the commodity which it nevertheless purports to denote.[20] It would be pointless to treat this as morally reprehensible and to blame individual producers. For within the given economic system, the functional determinants of the commodity (and of the brand-named product in particular) are quite rational in terms of realizing profit, and moreover market competition makes them compulsory.

The specific constitution of a brand-named product rests necessarily only on its image, which in turn becomes the basis for a monopoly price. Hence, in the case of evaporated milk – a uniformly manufactured product – in the Federal Republic alone there are 33 brands at 30 different prices, ranging from 74 Pfennig to DM1.28. At the top of the price range are three brands with the strongest national promotion – Libby, Glücksklee and Nestlé. These companies also supply the cheaper markets, i.e. the poorer or thriftier consumers, to whom they sell the same products cheaper under different labels and through subsidiaries.

Another example comes with the announcement of a verdict in the West German Federal Court, concerning the lifting of a fixed retail price for Melitta coffee filters. Melitta-Werke Benz in Minden distribute filters ('Melitta 102') at a fixed retail price of DM1.10 for 40. Their subsidiary, Ruf Import and Export MbH in Hamburg, markets the same packet under the name 'Brigitta Filter' at 75 Pf. This also happens in the case of noodles, rice, coffee powder and sparkling-wine labels. 'The "difference in quality" between sparkling wines often lies only in the name and label.'[21] The Federal wine regulations which came into force on 20 July 1971 show very clearly the relationship between the market structure and brand-name, in the example of wine. Unlike other brand-named articles, wine names appear to have a basis in reality, that is in their collective or individual vineyard. Until the new law came into force, there were about 36,000 names relating to some 72,000 hectares of vineyards. Since legislation the collective vineyards are required to have a minimum size of five hectares, the previous size being an average of two. As a consequence of the new legislation, a large proportion of the wine names disappeared. 'In the Rhineland Palatinate approximately 15,000 vineyard names from a total of 20,000 were struck from the register. In Hessen only some 150 remain out of more than 1,000.'[22]

The reason for this drastic 'agricultural clear-out' (*Das Weinblatt*) and 'spring cleaning' (*Der Spiegel*) of names which – as it appears to the individual's consciousness always adapting itself to the current economic requirements – creates order where there was previously a 'chaos of nomenclatures' (*Das Weinblatt*), lies in the changed market structure, which demands that the commodities assume oligopolistic characters. 'Discount shops, supermarket chains and department stores, which sell almost half of their bottles with vintage and place identification, cannot instigate million-pound advertising campaigns for such small batches,' as the individually named vineyards once did. 'They need "large quantities of standardized wine" with "attractive names"' (*Das Weinblatt*). Thus the law enforces a labelling which, formerly, could have been prosecuted as counterfeit, and throws light on the close relationship between promotional commodity styling and the counterfeiting of commodities.

The reports of 'mastering' and mixing voices, as an accepted practice in the record industry, especially as practised on 'stars' better known to the buying masses in other areas of show-business, read like accounts of counterfeiting in wine production.

Even before the sports star set foot in the studio, several playback tapes were ready, and canned orchestral music was prepared for mixing with the voice of Kilius [a German ice-skating starlet]. On one tape the rhythm had been recorded, on another the melody, and on a third the choir music. To enhance Kilius's voice, however, further subtle touches proved necessary. Although she sang powerfully, the voice sounded too shrill and harsh. Therefore, producer

Schmidt decided to 'soften the pitch' and cushion it with a more lush accompaniment. He had the . . . choir part doubled . . . But that was still not good enough for the producer. So he hired the choir-singer Brückner to lead Marika Kilius through the melody once again. The results were two-fold: for one thing, the professional singer was meant to help the ice-skater relax in front of the microphone, get her into the mood, and lead the vocals; and secondly the long-awaited, saleable fullness of sound was achieved, with the final recording a remix of Kilius twice, the choir twice and a female voice accompanying them in the background.[23].

Thus remixed, the record, *Wenn die Cowboys träumen,* quickly sold 300,000 copies through the American company CBS and was a commercial success, 'largely financed by secondary-school children's pocket money'.[24]

The buyer, who is trying to decide between competing brands, has a choice of names, shapes and images: to sellers wishing to remain in competition, these elements are all the more vital to survival. Court battles are fought over them, such as happened a few years ago, when the right to use the shape of the *Bocksbeutel* [like the Mateus Rosé bottle] was contested. The firm of Deinhard and Company, for example, is considering an allegation of unconstitutionality against the new wine law, since it comes into conflict with the 'right of proprietary possession'. Paragraph 59, Article 2 of this law explicitly prohibits the labelling of any beverage other than wine as *Kabinett, Spätlese* or *Auslese,* subject here to certain restrictions concerning the objective meaning of the words. It means that *Deinhard Cabinett* can no longer be marketed under its brand-name *Cabinett* after a statutory period of three years. Supported by legal advice from Professor Götz of Göttingen University, the firm is presenting an argument which casts light on the proprietorial basis of the name-structure of brand-named goods. 'The *Cabinett* brand-name was acquired for many millions of Deutschmarks, and enjoys the goodwill of consumers both here and abroad which would be destroyed by the removal of the name.'[22]

Spending out 'many millions' of Deutschmarks on a brand-name campaign, which entails appropriating and privatizing a word in common usage and consciousness and making it into a name exclusive to one's own commodity, is seen by the capitalist as a normal purchase, and what has thus been 'earned' is regarded self-evidently as a piece of private property. The words turned into brand-names by the campaign now become a part of the company's capital assets.

Where the battle between industrial giants is fought with and for names, it may happen that someone has to go to court over his or her own name; Rosemarie Heinicke of Munich did for the sake of her professional name, 'Rosy-Rosy'. The lady, 'well known for her bust size',[26] which is her trademark, not only sells glimpses of her physique but also samples of its form. She sells plastic prints of her bosom, technically reproduced and multiplied, thus not the bosom itself, but something which can be aesthetically – in this case plastically – detached and separately reproduced: its plastic appearance. Rosy-Rosy, whose name in the form of a nickname became the brand-name and her bosom the trademark, while its abstracted shape became the commodity, had to sue for possession of her own name, which was claimed by a textile mail-order firm in Pforzheim. The company maintained that it had been marketing 'sexy underclothes' under the trade name 'Rosy' for the last 22 years. What is remarkable about this contest is that here, as it were the packaging and the object to be packaged are disputing the brand-name; what was exposed by the name 'Rosy-Rosy' was to be covered up by the name 'Rosy', in a way which promises its stimuli through the packaging and thus stimulates desire in others. The Fourth Chamber of Commerce in the Darmstadt Regional Court, which had to consider the contest over names between the commodity and its packaging, rejected any danger of the two ever being confused and dismissed the suit.

Occasionally a firm will introduce a new article to compete with its own products in order to fend off outside competition by keeping it 'in the family'. Just such a manoeuvre gave the German public 'White Giant' by Henkel, who control approximately 50 per cent of the market in the Federal Republic in all-purpose washing powders. Henkel got wind of Colgate's intention to break into the German market under the brand name of 'White Knight'. So, quick as a flash, Henkel responded by having the trademark 'White Giant' brought into the arena and registering the name.

When the Americans entered the market, the epithet 'White' could no longer remain exclusive, and eventually the 'White Knight' project resulted in 'Knight Ajax'. In less than two years the American 'Knight' was withdrawn from this side of the Atlantic, as proof of the ferocity of promotional campaigns in a market where advertising costs for single products vary from 10 to 15% of turnover.[27]

Henkel creates its own 'competition' with its four brand names, Persil, Fakt, White Giant, Prodixan. Persil is only recognizable as such when in its packet; loose, it is just another washing powder. The food and luxury industries, which have by far the largest turnover of any sector, are particularly highly characterized by the name, form and image of their branded goods. 'To "improve turnover",,' in the jargon of bourgeois trade magazines, 'in this, more than in any other field, depends on the packaging.'[28]

From the individual commodity the apparent features of the successful brand-name spread to other commodities. The form that succeeds for radios or shavers, determines the shape of toasters and hair-dryers. All the apparent aesthetic features of the commodity converge in the image of capital in production, which in turn determines the characteristics of individual commodities. 'By "image" we understand, roughly speaking, the total impression, the total experience of all objects, services and facilities of a business.'[29] That this image is both the expression and the means for increasing market power, that it is in no way based on these same objects, services and facilities but, in the final analysis, solely on the calculation of 'scoring a hit' with the consumer, is supported by Bongard's formulation, according to which this 'image' is a 'psychological fact'.[30] 'Related and partly congruent concepts,' Bongard continues, 'are reputation, prejudice, stereotype, representation of the public, imagery or dominant image.'[31] None of these relates to an objective content.

One of the examples considered by Bongard is the very instructive case of the Federal German airline, Lufthansa. In the fifties they lacked any technology or service that might have distinguished them from foreign rivals. The German aircraft industry as such no longer existed, so Lufthansa were obliged to fly the same planes as other airlines. This situation of objective (technical, and in the face of international price-agreement, financial) uncompetitiveness, under conditions of ongoing competition, illustrates 'the importance of practically the only way by which Lufthansa could be distinguished from its foreign competition . . . precisely that of its "image".'[32]

The design of this 'total impression' was assigned to the Polytechnic of Design in Ulm, where designs for Braun had also appeared. There they styled the overall appearance of the planes, air-hostesses' uniforms, tickets and luggage labels, lunch boxes, and bills, timetables and departure gates. From the 'brand-technical point of view', which Bongard takes up explicitly on another occasion,[33] he criticizes Lufthansa for not carrying out the Ulm design in all its details. Even *Die Zeit,* the liberal weekly, passed judgement and advocated a styling of the Lufthansa image which took account of this 'brand-technique', as its 'only practical means of differentiating itself among the foreign competition.'[34]

The successful trademark – and its success transforms it to a certain extent into a monopoly commodity, since what succeeds is the original presentation which, as such, faces no competition – feeds back on its origin, the producing capital. From there it reflects back on to other commodities of the same origin. Commodities presented in such a fashion hardly compete in terms of use-value with rival products of other firms. Competition has widely shifted on to the level of images: now image fights image, incurring a drain on the national economy that runs into billions.[35] The successful technique of the monopolies overflows from the narrow economic field into the political. Thus it is self-evident to Bongard that the term 'image', as it describes the technique of monopolistic competition, 'can be applied to an economic enterprise just as much as to a political party, to a film star, or to a cake of soap, in short to any object whatsoever about which one can have an opinion.'[36] These 'objects of interest' can be any type of commodity, from the strictly brand-name standpoint whose reality is that of the advertising agency awaiting commissions. These commissions are what count, and the interest and economic power which lie behind them, as well as the determining functions.

From the point of view of manipulation technique, there is only one homogeneity of 'objects of opinion', since their manipulation is not concerned with their objective qualities, nor with their production or transformation, but with the opinion of the masses about them. Its object of labour is opinion, and it develops its instrument of labour from the conditions and tendencies of this object. Thus it is concerned with the reassembling and reprogramming of the driving forces and components of opinion, reinforcing them in a certain direction, weakening them in another.

The successful use of these techniques in the sphere of election campaigns can display a fascinating influence, as is shown in a speech given in 1970 by the then Defence Minister, Helmut Schmidt, to a group of market researchers.[37] This article is interesting precisely because it reflects the speaker's personal experience wholly unproblematically. In the mirror of Helmut Schmidt's consciousness, the field of political struggle appears as a market, the politician as having to sell himself and his Party policy. However, Schmidt continues, the politician is 'not in any market competition', a phrase which he explains by a comparison with the capitalist.

> It seems as if the politician is competing with another from a rival Party. But in reality it is often the case that, unlike the industrialist or he who produces cars and has to sell them on the market, the politician is not subject to the corrective influence of the other, the competitor. He is only in competition with the impression that the other makes on public opinion. When the latter 'scores more of a hit' with his arguments, that is, for him, competition. Then he has to think whether he should move in a different direction. This is a very limited form of competition.[38]

In this respect the opposition Schmidt sets up with the industrialist may not be tenable. On the contrary, the conditions and techniques of the 'hit', which Schmidt outlined for the politician, in the first instance concern monopolies and their commodities. What does it mean when competition limits itself to the competition of impressions? Evidently it is not the objective features of the rival offers which are in competition. Thus there is no competition of use-values. Primarily the contest is between the images of the competing offers and those who offer them. What is the function of these images and how are they created? 'Politicians have to make themselves electable at more or less regular intervals.' It may be a weakness, but in any case it is one of the foundations of a 'democracy', 'that the candidate for election must make himself electable and agreeable to those who are supposed to elect him.' How does one make oneself electable and agreeable? Evidently not by policies nor by objective achievements. 'Even someone who is successful will not be elected if he does not have enough charisma on television.' 'If for example somebody does not impress the viewers often it is not that person's own fault, and their actual abilities and character may play a quite insignificant part.'

It is of no importance, according to Schmidt's own experience (which at the same time he acknowledges to be the guideline for his action) who one is, what a certain party is, what is wanted and what is achieved. What counts is the image, the impression, 'scoring a hit'. How are the voters impressed? They are 'mostly informed – or hoodwinked – by the candidate they probably intend to vote for.' How can he hoodwink them? 'For this he has to understand their innermost desires and wishes.' What is articulated here with a naive lack of scruples is the 'standpoint of trademark-technique'. When 'scoring a hit' is decisive, the trademark-technique draws on the subjective requirements for the 'hit'. Neither social interests or needs, businesses, or class struggles enter the thoughts of the politician who tries to coordinate his campaign along the lines of trademark achievements. As little as the objective qualities and differences count in Helmut Schmidt's experience and attitudes, he reflects equally little upon the whys and wherefores of his own career of hits, whose forms of existence seem, to his sort of consciousness, to be completely independent.

Within the narrow scope of requirements for action and self-promotion, according to Schmidt's past and present experience, the belief in some phantom-like competition of impressions is quite correct and, what is more, has proved workable for individual careers. Also it cannot be denied that the technique of trademarks, since its development, has had a most powerful influence on politics. Gerhard Voigt has shown how Goebbels, in his technique of propaganda, can be conceived of as a technician of trademarks, having been greatly influenced by advertising experts, and not least by American capital.[39] 'It is only from the angle of these cynical, unscrupulous advertising techniques,' writes Lukács in *The Destruction of Reason,* 'that we can accurately portray the Hitler fascists' so-called ideology.'[40]

Voigt demonstrates how the characteristics of trademark monopolization played a substantial role in language control: 'Perhaps the
most rigid of Goebbels' language controls was the seizure of the
word "propaganda" for the political promotion of the NSDAP
and the Nazi state. Already, by the 27 October 1933, "propaganda"
as a Nazi concept was established in the "Second Directive to the
Legal Enforcement on Business Advertising" and its use was made
illegal for industry.' The Advertising Council of the German Trade
Department duly informed its members that 'commodity nomenclatures containing the word "propaganda", such as "Propaganda
Coffee" and "Propaganda Mixture", and so on' would no longer
be tolerated. 'Furthermore . . . the general use of the word
"propaganda" in business advertising must be deemed undesirable'. Voigt concludes: 'Precisely at this point, where the spheres of
politics and economy are separated, the identity of their methods
comes to light.'[41]

6   The unreality of commodity aesthetics vs the reality of
    promotional gifts; shop-lifting as the individual's reversal
    of promotional gifts

Despite a considerable identity of methods and phenomena, the
equation of a 'hit' in commodities with a 'hit' in political programmes and parties, as in Schmidt's experience, is a dubious one:
politics is not a consumable commodity nor is it sold.[42] If one talks
of politics having to be 'sold', it is in the first instance no more than
a metaphor borrowed from the jargon of advertising agents – or
rather from the jargon of advertisement *for* advertising. Firstly,
we would have to elaborate a comparative analysis of different
phenomena involved in scoring 'hits' – of courtship, poetry,
political agitation, propaganda and business advertising. Nevertheless, Schmidt has clearly sensed one dominant trait of monopoly
capital: the replacement of use-value competition by competition
of impressions, that is, the immense importance of techniques
designed to impress, against which the objective reality – as well
as the real interests of the people – are, to repeat Bongard's term,
mere 'objects of opinion'. Where mere competition of impressions
appears to determine the landscape of the sphere of circulation, it is

understandable that to critical observers the use-value of commodities seems to go astray.

> Compare the standard of today's department stores with the pre-1914 era. The decline in quality offered to the masses can be seen not only in the commodities themselves but in the way they are presented. The style of presentation, thanks to the perfecting of techniques which exploit the raw materials to the limit, is pushed to extreme refinement of the mere surface. The commodities offer, as in the style of Louis XV, an ever more shiny and shallow skin, which promises more and more while giving less and less. In the long run, experience cannot help but draw conclusions from poorer durability and earlier obsolescence; hence the increasingly hectic advertising campaigns. The commodities themselves provide less and less of what they actually should provide, in terms of a given system; if the buyers were not incessantly provided with ideological happiness too, the commodities themselves could hardly radiate emotional contentment either. Their real content becomes less and less substantial, and it is only a matter of time before the world of commodities reaches the point where it has to break with reality altogether.[43]

This point has long been passed in the illusory realm of commodity aesthetics, which does not mean however that the commodities no longer have any use-value at all; but that they really provide almost nothing of what they promise aesthetically. In so far as commodity aesthetics scores a 'hit' with the buyers, and determines their behaviour and, not least, their spending, the buyers are in a position similar to Tantalus, finding himself surrounded by the most beautiful delusions of his needs: when he reaches for them, he clutches empty space: 'Tantalus is the addicted buyer'.[44]

The dialectics of this functional vacuum, in the face of the addicted buyer who rushes headlong after mere images, finds its expression in the ostentatious completion of the promotional gift. An advertising consultant urgently warned in the *Industriekurier* of the 'great temptation to make the promotional gift, in its flashy appearance, seem to be more than it actually is'.[45] The particular target of the gilt-edged promotional gift can be the wholesale buyer, the 'business associate' of the firm, often in the person of, for example, the purchasing department boss, or of the head secretary of another firm, all of whom are themselves capitalist (or public) servants. It may be the copper-plated, party beer-barrel for him, or for her the silver handbag clasp. The intended 'advertising memento' is achieved through an exaggerated use-value which is tailor-made for the person in question. It is desirable that 'the character of the products or services to be advertised are represented in the promotional gift' but in an indirect, symbolic way rather than obtrusively explicit.

But the gilt-edged promotional gift creates its advertising effect precisely by denying its determining aim; according to its ideal, it is and is not what it is, like a Surrealist work of art. It is intended to represent the advertised firm or commodity, while at the same time it is only directed at one person – the target. To serve its purpose, it should ideally be extremely discreet, lest its target be moved to agree with the poet that 'to spot a deliberate intention puts one out of humour'. Consequently a manufacturer of promotional gifts has declared that 'the expression "promotional gift" should be prohibited completely.'[46] In the elevated, American-inspired language of camouflage, they are called 'contacts'. 'After all,' this same entrepreneur adds in modern camouflage, 'they are a means of communication!'[47]

The promotional gifts fulfil their function in a strange amalgam of *being* and *seeming*. They stand for and must represent something else. Yet their manner of representation is not mere seeming; it is the mode of being which represents. They fulfil their function 'by themselves representing usefulness'. By being useful and thus confirming their own use-value, they act as the promise of use-value of another product – the standard commodity of the donor. In this relationship between capitalists or capital agents, promise of use-value is cast towards to the prospective buyer, though not in the mode of mere seeming but in the mode of a being which is the representative of something else. The mere exaggerated illusion of use-value there, corresponds to the accentuated but heterogeneous use-value here. In the representational existence of the gift, the illusion is objectified: the seeming appears here precisely in the non-seeming. The representation of its completion should accompany the representation of the standard commodity of the donor.

The 'free-gifts' promotion has to be distinguished from the promotional gift. The former addresses itself directly to the consumer mass, the latter to capitalist wholesale buyers. The promotional gift flatters the capitalist wholesale buyer with the advertising completion of its representative use-value, while free gifts means distributing samples of brand-name goods to prospective individual buyers. Essentially, the free-gifts promotion distributes the image and packaging of brand-name articles; since empty packages would hardly be gratefully received, they contain tiny amounts of the corresponding use-value as a tangible stimulus.

One firm which capitalizes on this branch of advertising, the Felicitas Gift Service, addresses itself in particular to newly-weds. The firm 'has packaged "advertising" and "giving" into a ceremony which amplifies . . . the effect.'[48] It can be seen that in the pragmatic world view of the capitalist and hence in the theoretical view of the journalist, the concept of the promotional package can be transferred from the individual commodity to complex non-material processes, (here the handing over of advertising packages). The way this procedure is 'packaged' can be seen in the following description (which is given from a bourgeois, affirmative point of view). The trial packets are not just sent.

> The Frankfurt firm prefers to exploit the positive effects of the sentimental "first-name gambit". Some 400 hostesses, usually married and thus able to relate their own experiences to the ingenuous bride, visit newly married couples . . . In the course of conversation, the young bride is enlightened as to the advantages of the products in the Felicitas gift set. In order that the seeds may fall on fertile ground, the hostesses are selected according to strict specifications. They must not only be good-looking, but also charming, intelligent and adaptable.'[49]

While in this procedure free gifts are handed over, the looks, behaviour and conversation of the 'hostesses' serve as the living packaging of the procedure. In the place of mere packages, human beings are used to counteract any misgiving about mere packages. The 'first-name gambit' means that they are paid to act as packages, which appear to behave as independent-minded people who confide their experiences to you and are personally attractive. The humanity of these hostesses is calculated by capital to be the very illusion which deceives the consumer in the course of the free-gifts promotion. For the hostesses, it means that they hire out their physical and mental powers to capital, which assumes the expression of these human powers, dresses up in them, and appears to the buying masses in their guise as 'charming, intelligent and adaptable'.

It seems like both a caricature and a test of this example if one considers the unauthorized reversal of the promotional gift that the individual buyer has devised in a way that capital did not intend – shoplifting. Department stores and self-service shops in the Federal Republic anticipated a loss from shoplifting of between 800 million and one billion Deutschmarks in 1971.[50] According to statistics from the Federal Crime Bureau, 147,315 shoplifters were caught during 1970, i.e. 26.7 per cent more than in 1969, and almost four times as many as in 1963. At the Karstadt firm the number of detected thefts increased by 50 per cent. The company was prevailed upon to call a conference in Siegen to discuss the question of shoplifting, and hired Professor Wolfgang de Boor who runs an Institute for Research into Conflict in Cologne.

In the discussion of shoplifting, the functional complex of commodity aesthetics emerged as a central issue for the agents of capital, who were forcibly made to realize that people steal for exactly the same reasons as they normally would buy. Werner Heinl, Vice-President of the Federal Crime Bureau, expresses the relationship between commodity aesthetics and shoplifting by pointing out that one can 'frequently measure the quality of advertising in self-service shops by the number of thefts committed there.'[51] De Boor names 'the seductive offer, this provocative wealth', and concludes that 'both buyer and thief' succumb to the same impulse. In the booklet, *Fight Shoplifting,* issued by the Institute of Managerial Advice to the Retailer, Victor Scheitlin also sees the increase in shoplifting in 'the tendency in modern commodity presentation to make the offers so seductive that a spontaneous compulsion to purchase arises'. Added to this are the special features of the self-service store. Not only is 'the personal relationship between the perpetrator and proprietor no longer present in the supermarket', but also there is no 'service'. This means first and foremost no 'sales talk', instead, the commodities, the styling and displays, impersonally perform the selling functions themselves. Under these conditions, 'self-service' can become a synonym for appropriation without payment. The reason for this is obvious: the functional complex of commodity aesthetics is meant to trigger off the act of buying as forcefully as possible. Its functional ideal would be the compulsion to buy, but it is not capable of this directly. In so far as advertising directly commands us to buy, most people make purchases anyway. But if the 'desire to buy' could be induced directly, there would be no shoplifting problem.

Commodity aesthetics fulfils its function only via needs, which it must channel towards a certain commodity, and whip up into a compulsive intensity. The success of commodity aesthetics is the specific need, which irresistibly demands the acquisition of the 'courted' commodity. The form of acquisition remains indeterminate. It can only manufacture images to attract its targets, who are lusting after commodities. Thus not only the sales figures but also the theft rates are to be seen as an achievement of commodity aesthetics. [52]

7   The second effect of monopolization: aesthetic
    innovation – obsolescence of the current use-values;
    out with the old and in with the new; old records are
    boring! ties get broader; solution to the 1967 crisis in
    menswear: cowards wear grey; the young as ideal
    customers, hence the compulsion to appear young

With increasing productivity, the problem of profit realization for the oligopolies returns in a new guise. Now the productive forces of organized private capital no longer impinge on competing rivals so much as on their boundaries, directly on the limits of the relations of production, which define the demands of society, in so far as these demands bring purchasing power to bear. In a society like the USA, a large part of the total demand depends, as Baran and Sweezy have observed, 'on the need to replace a part of this stock of consumer durable goods as it wears out or is discarded.' [53] Since the way towards a total labour-saving society would amount to the abolition of capitalism, capital is now taking umbrage at the excessive durability of its products. One technique which answers this problem of in particular longer-lasting consumer durables like cars, electrical appliances, light bulbs and textiles, is to reduce the quality of the products. This technique has radically altered the standards of use-value in many areas of private consumption in favour of a shorter lifetime and lower resistance to wear.

The technique of reducing a commodity's useful life has been discussed under the concept of 'artificial obsolescence', which has been translated by the expression 'product senility'. The commodities enter the world with a kind of timing device which will trigger off their inner self-destruction within a calculated period.[54] Another technique is that of reducing the quantity being sold in an unaltered guise. A compromise between qualitative obsolescence and quantitative reduction of a product is shown in the way cloth is becoming thinner, etc. Commodities particularly suitable for quantitative reduction are foodstuffs and similar articles for private consumption which are sold in filled, brand-named packets.

When the price and styling of a carton of pasta, remain unchanged but the content is reduced, a new term in practical commodity selling appears – the concept of 'fill-level'. It describes the level to which the package is – just about – filled. The word appears specifically when the commodity's packet is regularly sold partially empty. Since the empty space, which makes the fill-level obvious, is open to conscious perception, certain firms have adopted the highly ingenious concealed device of a false bottom in the packaging. This was used by the Henkel corporation, whose brand of Khasana Creme 21 competed with Beiersdorf's Nivea: Henkel offered 150-cc tubs at DM2.90 which looked considerably bigger than the 150-cc Nivea tubs at DM2.60. The effect was achieved with an outwardly invisible cavity, 6–13 mm deep in the bottom of the tub. The law of action and reaction applies on the capitalist commodity market even more than in the world of physics. Beiersdorf introduced a Nivea tub on the market whose false bottom even outdid Henkel's; going by its image, the tub looks the same size as the 150-cc Henkel Khasana, but contains only 100 cc and costs DM2.50.[55]

As a rule, the reduction of use-value both in quality and quantity is compensated for by ornamentation. But even so, articles for use still last too long for capital's need for valorization. The more radical technique seizes not only upon a product's objective use-value, in order to shorten its useful life in the sphere of consumption and generate further demand prematurely: this technique starts with the aesthetics of the commodity. By periodically redesigning a commodity's appearance, it reduces the use-lifetime of the specific commodity, whose models are already functioning in the sphere of consumption. This technique, which we shall call aesthetic innovation, operates as follows: its full development and systematic application through the length and breadth of the commodity world, especially the sector for private consumption, requires the subordination of use-value to brand-name, thus in a sense ensuring the victory of the monopoly commodity, since every brand-name intends to set up an aesthetic monopoly. Nonetheless, aesthetic innovation, like other such techniques, is not historically speaking an invention of monopoly capitalism, but it emerges regularly wherever the economic function, which is at its root, arises.

Kulischer's *Allgemeine Wirtschaftsgeschichte* quotes instructions from the eighteenth century, which provide evidence that aesthetic innovation was already a quite consciously employed technique even then. A decree passed in 1755 for the cotton industry of Saxony reads that for the good of the 'Factory' – which here still meant craftshops, as production was still organized according to distributing firms (commodities were produced by individual pro-prietors for the capitalist wholesaler) – it was necessary that 'apart from the finer garments, the commodities themselves should be made to a new taste and design.'[56]

Note that the point is not the benefit of the buyers, as would be the case from the standpoint of use-value; rather, it is for the benefit of the entrepreneur, i.e. from the standpoint of exchange-value which is concerned with regenerating demand. Even though aesthetic innovation was not invented by monopoly capitalism, it is only within this system that it achieves a crucial meaning, dominating production in all decisive branches of the consumer-goods industry and playing a vital role in the capitalist organization of this industry. Never before was it manifested in such an aggress-ive manner. Like political slogans, posters in department-store windows announce the desires of capital, which command the customers. 'Out with the old and in with the new!', for example, was a slogan recently used by a furniture chain.

The record company, Polydor, with Deutsche Gramophon, managed by Siemens and Philips in the Polygram Syndicate, issued an advertising poster for retailers with the message, 'Old records are boring.' A picture, produced with all the tricks of the trade, plainly functioned as 'instructions for use': it showed the ruin of the 'old' records bent, burnt, melted, broken. This is the pipe-dream of monopoly.

The buyers experience the aesthetic innovation as an inevitable, although fascinating, fate. In the aesthetic innovation the commodities are driven by an inner dynamism, and appear as 'things which transcend sensuousness'. What appears here, reflected in the modification of the commodity's skin and body, is the fetish character of the commodity in its monopolistic peculiarity. The illusion is maintained that it is the things as such which change by themselves. 'Ties are getting broader and more colourful', writes a journalist in *Die Welt* in all seriousness.[57] If this utterly superficial statement is out of place in the business section of a newspaper whose editors should know better, it still adequately reflects what the buyers and users experience. Ties appear, like skirts, shirts, trousers, shoes, furniture, etc. as part of the *natura naturens* of the commodity world. The aesthetically differentiated generations of commodities replace one another, as if from natural causes, like changes in the weather. From the standpoint of the capitalists, the process looks completely different. For them it belongs to the realm, *natura naturata,* of their capital, which it is their business to produce amid anxiety and high risk. They require that the social 'necessity' – for such is the use-value of their commodities – be sanctioned again and again to achieve the determining aim of the valorization standpoint.

The masses of neckties at present in use – the 'tie wealth' of the society – are an obstacle, and a nightmare to the capital involved in this market. So its image-makers get the job of designing a new image for the tie, to try to create a new 'necessity' with the new fashion. According to their motive, aesthetic innovation is thus basically aesthetic ageing – they are not interested in the new as such. Their determining aim is the outdating of what exists, its denunciation, devaluation, and replacement. An unplanned economy directed by the profit motive compels this development.

In the wake of the 1966-7 recession in the west, an offensive of aesthetic innovation was launched in the menswear sector. 'This year the menswear industry suffered by far the biggest loss in turn-over in the whole clothing trade: up to DM600 million, a turnover of 20 per cent lower than the previous year (against a textiles' average of 10 per cent),' reported *Der Spiegel* in 1967.[58] 'The crisis hit an industry accustomed to triumphs, an industry which had trebled its sales since 1950, and had created large industrial concerns with a turnover of more than DM100 million.' The sector reacted with a feverish increase in the budget of their advertising section, Fertigkleidung GmbH. The investigation into the prevailing standard of use-value showed what everyone knew already: 'that the vast majority of the male population still did not want to "attract attention", but to look "timeless" and "serious".' As expressed and quantified by colour, 'around 60 per cent of the clothes,' says the report 'are grey.' The advertising section commissioned the Hamburg advertising agency, Gilde, to mount its offensive for aesthetic innovation or, more precisely, for the aesthetic ageing of the still wearable, and predominantly grey, clothes currently in fashion.

The result was slogans mobilizing the *anxiety* potential and aimed to undermine the then current standards of appearance of the sober, orderly and well-groomed bourgeois. 'Cowards wear grey,' they proclaimed. 'Old coats make you look fat!' 'Old suits make men appear tired!' 'Always wearing the same suit is like eating left-overs. Boring!' Old – meaning in concrete terms older than one season's fashion – and grey were to be equated with cowardly, fat, tired and boring.[59]

Here the aesthetic changes in the generations of commodities reach out to the people, changing their image along with that of the commodities. Under the pressure of the crisis, the profit mechanism produces a tendency which keeps the image of what is masculine and manly in a state of flux. Yet the process has another dimension which determines the lives of millions of people. 'Only about 2 per cent, of mainly young people' admitted to favouring highly fashionable clothes (in Germany) in 1967, and they bought from boutiques which mainly imported the commodities from abroad. Hence the campaign for the aesthetic innovation of menswear had to start with these 'ideal customers'.

By initiating a new commodity generation of suits, shirts and jackets, the campaign at the same time promoted the youthfulness of these ideal customers. A portion of youth subculture provided the aesthetic basis on which the clothing industry, by means of a new generation of commodities, managed to overcome the economic crisis. Simultaneously it advertised youthfulness as essential to the new standardized image. The natural characteristics of whole generations of men became outdated along with the obsolete generation of commodities. Youth fetishism and the compulsive character of the young originate in one respect in this aesthetic innovation, which is only an expression of and a technique for coping with a situation in which the relations of production have become a decisive fetter on the productive forces. This technique for coping has helped to establish the dominance of the irrationality in this society over even the smallest things in everyday use.

In the textile, car and food industries,[60] for household appliances, books, drugs and cosmetics, regular aesthetic innovations, which turn use-value over and over are enough to make the user dizzy: to insist on the standpoint of use-value under such conditions is almost impossible. This tendency is inevitable within capitalism, but it is only the smallest evil that capitalism has to offer today. As long as fascism and war do not suddenly increase the demand for military commodities, and the productive forces no longer threaten to burst asunder the narrowed boundaries of the relations of production, aesthetic innovation will be securely rooted within an oligopolistic-structured capitalist society. It subjects the whole world of useful things, in which people articulate their needs in the language of commercial products, to an incessant aesthetic revolution in the course of their inclusion in monopoly capitalist commodity production.

Aesthetic innovation, as the functionary for regenerating demand, is thus transformed into a moment of direct anthropological power and influence, in that it continually changes humankind as a species in their sensual organization, in their real orientation and material lifestyle, as much as in the perception, satisfaction and structure of their needs.

Chapter Two

---

1   The technocracy of sensuality – in general

With the aid of examples, we can now investigate and at least outline how and in what form human sensuality is moulded by commodity aesthetics, how sensuality for its part reacts to this, and how human need and instinct structures are altered under the impact of a continuously changing prospect of satisfaction offered by commodities. Before this, however, we need to consider one particular aspect of human domination over nature – the domination of and arbitrary and unlimited illusory reproductibility of nature's appearance. But what we have called here the technocracy of sensuality means more than this kind of domination. It means domination over people that is effected through their fascination with technically produced artificial appearances. This domination thus does not appear directly but lies in the fascination of aesthetic images. Fascination means simply that these aesthetic images capture people's sensuality. In the course of dominating one's sensuality, the fascinated individual is dominated by his or her own senses.

In Plato's famous parable of the cave the moments of such a state of fascination are present, but *cui bono*? The use that the person in control gains from this relationship of domination is completely obscured by abstract philosophizing. The extreme artificiality and technical expertise in the situation as described by Plato have mostly gone unnoticed:

> Behold! human beings housed in an underground cave, which has a long entrance open towards the light and as wide as the interior of the cave; here they have been from their childhood, and have their legs and necks chained, so that they cannot move and can only see before them, being prevented by the chains from turning round their heads. Above and behind them a fire is blazing at a distance, and

between the fire and the prisoners there is a raised way; and you will
see, if you look, a low wall built along the way, like the screen which
marionette players have in front of them, over which they show the
puppets . . . And do you see . . . men passing along the wall carrying
all sorts of vessels, and statues and figures of animals made of wood
and stone and various materials, which appear over the wall? While
carrying their burdens, some of them, as you would expect, are talking, others silent.[1]

The aim of this arrangement, of course, is that the shadows of the
monsters carried past are projected on to the wall as on to a screen,
and are mistaken by the people, who are captured by the illusion,
for moments of reality itself. Hence, also, the words of the
stewards passing behind their backs are attributed to the fetish-like
silhouettes projected by the artificial light in the background. The
fact that the captives are fettered is merely added to illustrate that,
fascinated as they are, they would stay seated, staring at the screen,
even without these additional bindings. Even if untied, they would
violently resist the urge to turn and see through the artifice, which
would mean taking their first step towards freedom and truth.

The technocracy of sensuality as a means of acquiring the products of other people's labour, generally in the cause of social and
political domination, is no more an invention of capitalism than is
fetishism. The stage appearance is not conceivable outside the
history of cults. One need only remind onself of the vast aesthetic
of magic in the Catholic churches and places of pilgrimage in the
late Middle Ages, which were both an expression of, and an attraction for wealth. With the piligrims came a part of the surplus product, to be skimmed off in the form of fees for rituals of all kinds,
sacrifices, pious donations, and the like. Once again an exercise in
appearance is carried out, this time by the Church, in order to make
money.

Or consider the Counter-Reformation, that cultural struggle
fought with all the resources of theatre, architecture, and painting,
by the old power of the church which felt threatened by the rising
powers of bourgeois society. Its fundamental difference from the
illusion-making of capitalism lies, of course, in the fact that in
capitalism it is primarily the valorization functions which adopt,
modify and develop the aesthetic techniques. The result is no longer

restricted to specific holy places or to those representing power, but forms a totality of the sensual world, of which even the smallest part has now been put through capitalist valorization processes, and been indelibly marked by their functions.

2   The high status of mere illusion in capitalism

The production and great importance of mere illusion are rooted in capitalist society in the fundamental contradiction which permeates it at all levels, and whose development from the exchange-value relation we traced at the beginning of this enquiry. Capitalism is based on a systematic *quid pro quo*: all human goals, even life itself, matter only as means and pretexts (not just in theory but in economic fact) in the functioning of the system. The standpoint of capital valorization as an end in itself, to which all human endeavours, longings, instincts and hopes are just exploitable means, (and motivations which people can relate to and on whose research and usage a whole branch of the social sciences is working), this valorization standpoint which dominates absolutely in capitalist society, is diametrically opposed to what people are and want autonomously. Taken in the abstract, the mediation between people and capital can thus be but an illusion: of necessity, capitalism is rooted in this illusory world. In other words, the generality of human goals under capitalism, so long as they are content to remain under its control, can never be more than a bad illusion which, nevertheless, attains a high status in such a society.

The valorization standpoint of capital pursues its claim to absolute domination in an ambivalent relationship to the sensuality of the human being. In so far as this being puts up resistance to the domination of capital, human independence is destroyed by it; and in so far as the domination of capital is mediated by moments of sensual and instinctual life, these elements are persistently made to seem dependent and incongruous. The individuals whom capital conditions to be either its functionaries, capitalists themselves, or its wage labourers, share, at least formally, a common instinctual fate in spite of their radical differences: their sensual immediacy must be disrupted and rendered absolutely controllable. Unless people are driven to work for others by brute force, this is only possible if one natural urge is directed against another; for example, the illusion of a controlled sensuality is employed as a reward for conforming. For it is not only the great goals of humanity which become lost in the reality of capitalism, and therefore have to be recaptured through the medium of illusion, but this applies also to the individual's instinctual aims.

3   Aesthetic abstraction, philosophical foreplay

Now we need to investigate more deeply the structure, effect, and dynamics of the capitalistic use of illusion. The abstraction of use-value, as a consequence of and precondition for the establishment of exchange-value and its standpoint, paves the way for corresponding abstractions, which will make them both theoretically and above all practically valorizable. The functional vacuum, that is to say the demand of the system, is there even before the capabilities needed to fill it exist.

One of these abstractions is fundamental to the natural sciences, i.e the abstraction of use-values into qualities, for example, detaching the mere spatial extension of objects so that they become just that – mere *res extensae* – reduced at the same time to comparable quantity relations. It seems logical that Descartes, the pioneer of this abstract theoretical thought, should introduce aesthetic abstraction into the technique of de-realizing the sensual reality of the world. He makes the assumption that there is an almighty god of manipulation who, by means of some omnipresent television programme for the gullible, deceives the whole sensual world. Here, all shapes, colours, sounds, and 'all externals', are only a delusion. 'Myself,' he writes, 'I will regard as someone with neither hands nor eyes, neither flesh nor blood, nor any senses,'[2] but merely as a consciousness deceived by a technique in every way superior to humankind.

Descartes also gives more prosaic examples which amount to the same thing. First, a figure of given shape and colour, when held close to the heat, begins to melt, changes form and hue, and proves to be wax or some such plastic material which can be moulded into all kinds of sensual forms. Second, someone in the street walks past the window and for all we know it could easily be an automaton disguised in human clothes.[3]

All these examples and assumptions are intended to introduce the doctrine, henceforth termed a science, that in the first place only one thing is certain: that the processes of consciousness themselves do exist, but that their content can be falsified. Thus people are reduced to these falsifiable processes of consciousness. But what of inanimate objects? They are reduced to something 'extended in space, but flexible, and mutable' (*Extensum, quid flexibile, mutabile*).[4]

This is not the moment to develop the involuntary dialectic in this kind of early bourgeois theory, which begins with the aim of emancipating the individual from deception (especially pre-bourgeois deception), and ends with mere domination on one side and deception on the other. Instead, it is crucial to consider within the mediating context of economic and technological developments, that process we have introduced as 'aesthetic abstraction'.

4 Aesthetic abstraction of the commodity: surface – package – advertising image

The contradiction of interests between buyer and seller, use-value and exchange-value (or valorization), which ultimately dominates the unleashed commodity–cash nexus, exposes the object of use, which was made and acts as a carrier of value, to a field of antagonistic forces: in this dissection, to which the commodity is subjected under the calculated control of the valorization standpoint, the commodity's surface appearance and its meaning detach themselves and form a hybrid which performs a highly specific function. This hybrid is the expression, and carries out the function, of a social relationship as it appears in the relationship of the character-masks worn by buyer and seller. This antagonistic relationship constitutes the function: the economic function in turn leads to the emergence of the techniques and phenomena which become their carrier. In concrete terms this process can be imagined as a situation where everything functional contributes to phenomenal economic successes, which, once established and consciously repeated, go on to cripple economically anything which does not further this development. The function leading to the aesthetic abstraction of the commodity is realization, which, through the aesthetic promise of use-value, creates the means that trigger the sale.

The aesthetic abstraction of the commodity detaches both sensuality and meaning from the object acting as a carrier of exchange-value and makes the two separately available.[5] At first the functionally already separate form and surface, which already have their own manufacturing processes, remain with the commodity to develop as naturally as skin covers a body. Yet functional differentiation is preparing the actual process of replacement, and the beautifully designed surface of the commodity becomes its package: not the simple wrapping for protection during transportation, but its real countenance, which the potential buyer is shown first instead of the body of the commodity and through which the commodity develops and changes its countenance, like the fairytale princess who is transformed through her feathered costume in which she seeks her forture in the marketplace.[6] As an example of this, a US bank, in order to facilitate the exchange of money, recently changed even the design of its cheques to make use of new psychedelic colours.

But to return to the commodity: now that its surface has been detached and become its second skin, which as a rule is incomparably more perfect than the first, it becomes completely disembodied and drifts unencumbered like a multicoloured spirit of the commodity into every household, preparing the way for the real distribution of the commodity. No one is safe any longer from its amorous glances, which the realization motive casts at the consumers with the detached yet technically perfect appearance of a highly promising use-value.[7]. For the time being at least, the customers' wallets still hold the equivalent of this disguised exchange-value.

5   The mirror image of desire as deceptive illusion

Appearance always promises more, much more, than it can ever deliver. In this way the illusion deceives. There is a tale from *The Arabian Nights* which refers to this type of beautiful illusion, which actually traps people in the literal sense, and this tale demonstrates meaningfully illusion's links with trade capital. It is the story of the City of Brass.[8]

Surrounded by high walls of black stone, its gates so well concealed that they cannot be distinguished from the wall, the City of Brass, so named because of its Andalusian brass roofs, stands in the middle of the desert like a safe filled with the commodity capital of luxury goods. Since no way in can can be found, the Caliph's emissaries build a ladder. One of them climbs up,

> but, when he came to the top of the wall, he stood up and gazed fixedly down into the city, then clapped his hands and cried out at the top of his voice 'By Allah, thou art fair!', whereupon he cast himself down into the city and his body was broken into pieces. Said Emir Musa, 'If such be the action of a reasonable man, what would a madman do?'

One after another the emissaries climbed up, and the scene was repeated until twelve had been lost. Eventually the only one who knew the route to the city and back, Sheikh Abd al-Samad, mounted the ladder, for he was 'a man of varied knowledge who travelled much . . . a very ancient man . . . made frail with the passing of time.' If he too were to 'fall' into the trap, the whole delegation would be lost. So he climbed the ladder

> calling on the name of Allah and reciting Verses of Salvation. When he reached the top of the wall, he clapped his hands and stared fixedly down into the city; whereupon the folk below cried out . . . 'O Sheikh Abd al-Samad, for the Lord's sake, cast not thyself down!' . . . Then he laughed louder and louder and sat a long hour.

Later the Sheikh explained how he was not deceived by the illusion: 'As I stood on the wall I saw ten maidens like Houris of Heaven, and they were calling and waving – Come hither to us; and meseemed there was below me a lake of water.' But thanks to his piety, and even more to his age, the erotic mirage – overwhelming in a society where women went veiled – was dissolved. 'Doubtless,' the tale concludes, 'this was an enchantment devised by the people of the city, to repel any who should seek to gaze upon or to enter the place.'

This deceptive illusion is devised here from the standpoint of owning exchange-value. The fall is into the clutches of sexual desire. Those who jump down are gullible believers in use-value. Yet the story of the City of Brass exposes another level of the contradiction between use-value and exchange-value: this time it is of the fall of those acting from the standpoint of exchange-value. For the city is peopled only with shrivelled corpses, and the story reveals the reason why: in the midst of their immeasurable exchange-value, the owners ultimately lacked the bare necessities of life (use-values). For seven years it had not rained, the vegetation had withered, and the people had all starved to death.

The illusion one falls for is like a mirror in which one sees one's desires and believes them to be real. The people, as in monopoly capitalist society, are faced with a commodity world of attractive and seductive illusion and here, despite the outrageous deception, something very strange occurs, the dynamics of which are greatly underestimated. An innumerable series of images are forced upon the individual, like mirrors, seemingly empathetic and totally credible, which bring their secrets to the surface and display them there. In these images, people are continually shown the unfulfilled aspects of their existence. The illusion ingratiates itself, promising satisfaction: it reads desires in one's eyes, and brings them to the surface of the commodity. While the illusion with which commodities present themselves to the gaze, gives the people a sense of meaningfulness, it provides them with a language to interpret their existence and the world. Any other world, different from that provided by the commodities, is almost no longer accessible to them.

How can people behave, or change themselves, when continually presented with a collection of dream-images that have been taken from them? How can people change when they continue to get what they want, but only in the form of illusion? Commodity aesthetics' ideal would be to invent something which enters one's consciousness unlike anything else; something which is talked about, which catches the eye and which cannot be forgotten; something which everyone wants and has always wanted. Encountering little resistance, the consumer is being served, be it by way of the latest, and the most sensational, or the most modest, the most comfortable of things. Thus both greed and laziness are cultivated with equal care.[9]

6 Corrupting use-values: their feedback to the structure of needs

Commodity aesthetics, by determining the direction an individual's being takes, seems to warp the progressive tendency in human instincts, their desire for satisfaction, enjoyment, and happiness. Human motivation appears to have been shackled to a drive towards conformism. Many critical observers of contemporary culture see this as an all-embracing corruption of the entire species. Gehlen speaks of its degeneration as it adjusts to 'all-too-convenient living conditions'. Indeed, there is a deceitfulness in the servile flattery of commodities; their dominant tendency is the desire to serve in this way. Those served by capitalism are, in the end, unconsciously its servants – not merely pampered, distracted, fed and bribed by it.

In Brecht's didactic play, *Badener Lehrstück vom Einverständnis*, he investigates whether people actually help one another.[10] The third enquiry, a clown sketch, shows what happens when capitalism helps the individual – only, in this case, help means amputation. If you sit down you might never stand up again. Help means creating and thoroughly exploiting a dependency. Such is the dynamic of late-capitalist commodity production. First new commodities make the necessary chores that much easier, and then the chores become too difficult to do unaided, without inevitably buying the commodities. Now what is necessary cannot be distinguished from what is unnecessary but which one can no longer do without. The play's speech on false needs probably refers precisely to this displacement.

Do instincts and needs still have any progressive value under these conditions? Does any essential trace of people's material needs still remain? That which has occasionally been called repressive satisfaction now appears as corrupting use-value. In particular this dominates the area of illusion which concerns commodities. The corrupting use-value feeds back to the needs-structure of the consumers, whom it brings down to a corrupt standpoint of use-value. These corrupting influences, although only a side-effect of the dynamics of capitalist profit, are catastrophic to an almost anthropological extent. People seem to have had their consciousnesses bought off. They are conditioned daily to enjoy that which betrays them, to celebrate their own defeat, in the enjoyment of identifying with their superiors. Even the genuine use-values they receive, carry within them a tremendous power of destruction. The private car, together with the running-down of public transport, carves up the towns no less effectively than saturation bombing, and creates distances that can no longer be crossed without a car.

It would be pointless and premature to describe this process in terms of a systematic theory for corrupting the masses. For the ideal of commodity aesthetics is to deliver the absolute minimum of use-value, disguised and staged by a maximum of seductive illusion, a highly effective strategy because it is attuned to the yearnings, and desires, of the people. But despite commodity aesthetics' ideal, real use-value (whose effects require separate investigation), does not disappear. This contradiction is contained in commodity aesthetics as such. The agents of capital cannot do what they like with it, but rather they are dependent on the condition that they create, or appear to create, what the consumers want.

The dialectic of master and slave within the flirtation of commodity aesthetics remains ambiguous: certainly, capital dominates in the sphere where commodity aesthetics plays a role in affecting public consciousness and behaviour, and finally, worms its way in via the exchange-value in their pockets; thus a seemingly servile power becomes in effect dominant. Of course those who are supposedly served are being subjugated. But the fact that the dominance through a corrupting and illusory service creates its own dynamic can be illustrated by examining the consequences caused by using sexual illusion as a commodity in its own right, as well as the sexualization of many other commodities.

7   The ambiguity of commodity aesthetics exemplified by
     the use of sexual illusion

The ambiguity of commodity aesthetics is shown by its use of the sexually stimulating illusion. As we have already seen, it is a means of solving certain problems in valorization and capital realization. At the same time it is only an illusory solution to the contradiction of use-value and exchange-value.

Sex as a commodity appears at historically different, and very disparate, stages of development. Prostitution remains on the level of simple commodity production, or rather a service industry, with the pimp as capitalist agent and the brothel as factory. What all these forms of sexual commodification have in common is that their use-value is still realized in direct sensual or physical contact. Sexuality is only valorizable at an industrial capitalist level in the form of aesthetic abstraction – if one overlooks certain necessary props. The mere picture or sound, or a combination of both, can be recorded and reproduced on a mass basis, on a technically unlimited scale, which is restricted in practice only by the market.

In a situation of general sexual repression, or at least of isolation, the use-value of mere sexual illusion lies in the satisfaction which voyeurism can provide. This satisfaction through a use-value, whose specific nature is as an illusion, can be called illusory satisfaction. The characteristics of this satisfaction through sexual illusion is that it simultaneously reproduces further demand alongside satisfaction, and produces a compulsive fixation. If guilt feelings and the *angst* they arouse block the way to the sexual object, then the commodity of sexual illusion acts as its replacement, mediating excitement and a certain satisfaction which might be difficult to develop in actual sensual and physical contact. This type of seemingly unhindered satisfaction threatens to cut off completely the possibility of direct pleasure. Here the form of use-value as specifically employed for large-scale valorization feeds back on to the structure of needs. Thus a general voyeurism is reinforced, habituated, and determines the human instinctual structure.

The suppression of instincts plus the simultaneous illusory satisfaction of instincts tend towards a general sexualization of the human condition, called by Max Scheler *Gehirnsinnlichkeit* or 'sensuality on the brain'. The response of the commodities is to reflect sexual images from all sides. Here it is not the sexual object which takes on the commodity form, but the tendency of all objects of use in commodity-form to assume a sexual form to some extent. That is, the sensual need and the means by which it is satisfied are rendered non-specific. In a certain way, they come to resemble money, which Freud compared with anxiety in this respect:[11] triggered by almost anything, they become freely convertible into stimulation from any source. Thus by taking on sexuality as an assistant, exchange-value transforms itself into sexuality. All manner of goods are enveloped by its surface, and this background of sexual enjoyment becomes the commodity's most popular attire, or perhaps the gilded backdrop against which the commodity appears. The general sexualization of commodities has also included people. It provides an outlet for expressing previously suppressed sexual urges. Adolescents, most of all, make use of this possibility, and their demand generates a further supply. With the help of new fashions it is possible to advertise oneself as, above all, a sexual being.

Inherent in all this lies a remarkable return to our socio-historical point of departure. Just as the commodities once borrowed their seductive language from people, so now they return in a language of clothes conveying sexual feelings. And, even though the capital in the textile industry makes a profit from this, the power of the tentatively developing sexual liberation will not be restricted unconditionally again.[12]

So long as the economically determined function of commodity aesthetics exists, and continues to be driven by the profit motive, it will retain its ambiguous tendency: by serving people, in order to ensure *their* service, it brings an unending stream of desires into the open. Seen merely as commodity aesthetics, it can offer only an illusory satisfaction, which does not feed but causes hunger. And as a false solution to the contradiction, commodity aesthetics reproduces the contradiction in another form, which is perhaps even more far-reaching.

Chapter Three

1   The sales-talk – the roles of buyer and seller

Before the aesthetic promise of use-value breaks away, at first as a package and finally as an advertising image, it has an independent existence outside the commodity which can be traced to the verbal and non-verbal behaviour of the seller. Prior to the establishment of the industrial capitalist mass commodity, whose distribution system is suited to the requirements of a mass turnover, a large part of the functions of commodity aesthetics (later to be carried out in an entirely impersonal way) appear in the performances of those who have donned the 'character-mask' of the seller. 'Montesquieu, paying a visit to the Palais de Justice, had to pass "an endless crowd of young salesgirls who were trying to entice him with flattering words".'[1]

At the beginning of the eighteenth century, Mandeville in his *Fable of the Bees, or Private Vices – Public Benefits*, depicts with great skill 'the negotiations between a draper and a young lady who came to buy from him', and he investigates 'the above-mentioned people in turn regarding their inner thoughts and the differing motives for their behaviour.' The trader's business

is to sell as much silk as he can at a price by which he shall get what he proposes to be reasonable according to the customary profits of the trade. As to the lady, what she would be at is to please her fancy, and buy cheaper by a groat or sixpence per yard than the things she wants are commonly sold at. From the impression the gallantry of our sex has made upon her, she imagines (if she be not very deformed) that she has a fine mien and easy behaviour, and a peculiar sweetness of voice; that she is handsome, and if not beautiful at least more agreeable than most young women she knows. As she has no pretensions to purchase the same things with less money than other people, but what are built on her good qualities, so she sets herself off to the best advantage her wit and distinction will let her. The thoughts of love are here out of the case; so on the one hand she has no room for playing the tyrant, and giving herself angry and peevish airs, and on the other more liberty of speaking kindly, and being affable than she can have almost on any other occasion . . .

Before her coach is yet quite stopped, she is approached by a gentleman like man, that has everything clean and fashionable about him, who in low obeisance pays her homage, and as soon as her pleasure is known that she has a mind to come in, hands her into the shop, where immediately he slips from her and through a by-way, that remains visible only for half a moment, with great address entrenches himself behind the counter: here facing her, with a profound reverence and modish phrase he begs her favour of knowing her commands. Let her say and dislike what she pleases, she can never be directly contradicted: she deals with a man in whom consummate patience is one of the mysteries of his trade, and whatever trouble she creates, she is sure to hear nothing but the most obliging language, and has always before her a cheerful countenance, whose joy and respect seem to be blended with good humour, and altogether make up an artificial serenity more engaging than untaught nature is able to produce.

When two persons are so well met, the conversation must be very agreeable, as well as extremely mannerly, though they talk about trifles. Whilst she remains irresolute what to take, he seems to be the same in advising her; and is very cautious how to direct her choice; but when once she has made it and is fixed, he immediately becomes positive, that it is the best of the sort, extols her fancy, and the more he looks upon it the more he wonders he should not before have discovered the pre-eminence of it over anything he has in his shop. By precept, example and great application he has learned unobserved to slide into the inmost recesses of the soul, sound and the capacity of his customers, and find out their blind side unknown to them: by all which he is instructed in fifty other stratagems to make her over-value her own judgment as well as the commodity she would purchase.

The greatest advantage he has over her, lies in the most material part of the commerce between them, the debate about the price, which he knows to a farthing, and she is wholly ignorant of: therefore he nowhere more egregiously imposes on her understanding: and though here has the liberty of telling what lies he pleases, as to the prime cost and the money he has refused, yet he trusts not to them only; but attacking her vanity, makes her believe the most incredible things in the world, concerning his own weakness and her superior abilities. He had taken a resolution, he says, never to part with that piece under such a price, but she has the power of talking him out of his goods beyond anybody he ever sold to: he protests that he loses by his silk, but seeing that she has a fancy for it, and is resolved to give no more, rather than disoblige a lady he has such an uncommon value for, he will let her have it, and only begs that another time she will not stand so hard with him.

In the meantime the buyer, who knows that she is no fool and has a voluble tongue, is easily persuaded that she has a very winning way of talking, and thinking it sufficient for the sake of good breeding to disown her merit, and in some witty repartee retort the compliment, he makes her swallow very contentedly the substance of everything he tells her.

The upshot is, that with the satisfaction of having saved ninepence per yard, she has bought the silk exactly at the same price as anybody else might have done, and often gives sixpence more than, rather than not have sold it, he would have taken.[2]

The character-mask of the seller depicts flattering servitude and devotion above a studiedly fashionable appearance. The buyer's weak points are ignorance coupled with a belief in her own talents. Accordingly, an admiration for these imagined skills, and the pretence of being impressed by them, are part of the seller's act. He impresses precisely by pretending to be impressed; his technique takes the form of a flattering echo. His manner towards the buyer reflects a consistent servility, and the emotions which are functionally appropriate to his standpoint to reinforce the client's attitude.

Both character-masks of the draper and of his young customer are determined by their distance from the sphere of production. Both are non-producers. He is merely a tradesman, the incarnation of the sales function, and she is a luxury consumer. In this relationship of two non-producers, the asymmetry of their positions is enhanced by their fixed role-division and their distance from production. A sales talk between two producers proceeds more symmetrically. Where the character-masks have not yet been fixed by the division of labour, and are not stuck to certain people for life as if they had been born with them, the behaviour of each party is more adequately reciprocal. Yet this is not to say that in a more symmetrical relationship there is less illusion involved.

A portrait of the character-mask of the cautious buyer is given in a *Trainingskurs für Verkäufer* [*Training Course for Sales Assistants*].[3] Under the heading, 'The wary customer. How to spot and deal with them', their mannerisms and gestures are characterized first: 'Little movement; inhibited (Don't give yourself away) . . . hesitant; cautious; with furrowed brows'. The social situation is thus determined where two salesmen meet – the sales representatives of the wholesaler and of the retailer. Accordingly, the verbal expressions of the wary customer appear: 'reserved and hesitant, laconic but suddenly bursting out with unexpected questions, cross-examining the other.' *In toto*, his behaviour appears 'sensitive, alert, sceptical, reserved, uncompromising, full of scruples and doubts'. The monotony of these characteristics is based on the 'objective' character-masks evoked in the social relationship between sale and purchase.

Such characteristics on the part of the wary customer lead to the following 'treatment' recommended by the trained salesman: 'Do not push, take your time, be understanding . . . appear open, clear, correct, cheerful, optimistic, convince them with real arguments and win back their trust.' The scene is completely determined by reciprocal scrutiny, and the one-sided play-acting which the other side already anticipates from the start: the first party responds to this with a renewed pretence at openness personified, clarity and good-humoured optimism. This openness is of all the masks the most impenetrable.

Even before buyer enters the shop he is already categorized as a type, and the sales-talk with all its variations for different types is planned systematically in advance. His projected comments are anticipated as signals, to which answer must be made in a form which gives the best advantage to the valorization standpoint. Such pre-programmed sales-talk can only be an illusion of the form the conversation will take: in fact it is a struggle, more than anything else, in which only one protagonist knows that battle has commenced – and acts accordingly. Maintaining the buyer's ignorance, in such a one-sided struggle, has top priority in the seller's strategy. Part of this involves introducing and maintaining objects of perception which are peripheral to the central economic process of commodity-cash exchange, and which seem to follow a different set of rules. The further the commodity-cash nexus (the main sales determinant from the standpoint of trade capital) is pushed to the edge of the consumer's consciousness, the more indeterminate the character-mask of the buyer becomes, and the less his or her behaviour and attentiveness are influenced by its characteristics.

Lurking more and more conspicuously behind the mask is the emotional and foolish faith of those who are blinded by the illusion. In this social relationship in which the valorization standpoint dominates, a human being who needs something is interpreted as a 'consumer'; and the 'consumer' mask under which the buyer's conflict of interests (expressed by the character-mask) is hidden is an important component of that unconscious existence, which has been worked for from the standpoint of valorization with the greatest dedication.

Just as the mass media impose a language on the whole of the society whereby workers are only 'taking work' [*Arbeitnehmer*] and buyers are called consumers, similarly great pains are taken in sales-talk with learning a language in which it would be unthinkable to defend the interests of the buyer. The relevant instructional literature for salesmen inculcates the use of anaesthetizing verbal control which is expressly intended to gag the buyer behind a character-mask. 'Some shopkeepers forbid their sales staff to use the word "sell" at any time.'[4] Words like 'money', 'contract' and 'signature' are subject to the same taboo, the strategy being to give an illusion of indifference, in the interests of the ruling class. 'Contract', in the seemingly helpful language turns into 'entitlement'. 'Signature' becomes

> 'Please be so kind as to put your first and second names where I've marked with a cross.' And, as the form is handed over, 'Please press hard, because of the carbon copies, you know!' Mentioning the cross, first and second names, pressing hard, carbon copies, harmlessly occupies the buyer's thoughts, distracting attention from the fact that a legally binding signature is being given.[5]

Thus the sales instructor, Stangl, explains his recommended technique for controlling the language and the buyer's perception during the sales-talk.

The systematic vagueness and inconsequentiality of the sales talk is in stark contrast to their main objective, as evidenced by the advertising with which companies address retailers, or the mass media approach advertisers. 'Skim off the cream, too!' the dairy company B & B advertised in a trade journal.[6] Even the Catholic Diocesan and the Protestant Sunday press seek advertisers, hinting that a religious demeanour, inspired by the pious texts and biblical quotations in the paper's editorial, could stretch to the relationship to the advertisements.[7]

With the formation of the economically opposed character-masks of buyer and seller, an illusory solution of this conflict of interests emerges from the seller's side, even where no particular persons are as yet involved. An enthusiasm for the use-value of the commodity, as depicted in the above sales-talk, belongs to the mask of the seller as a euphoric skin which covers a deep anxiety over realization of its exchange-value. This masked enthusiasm is countered by the buyer who does not wish to appear stupid, with the consistent mistrust that marks his economic character-mask. Above these roles, which are based on the contradiction of exchange, abilities develop in the interplay of interests – optimistic praise and opposed denigration – which detach themselves from the act of exchange and ascend into the literary or even religious superstructure. The cultivation of personal sales-talk reaches the peak of these achieve-ments in simple commodity production.[8] As a general phenomenon it becomes stunted in its capitalist development.[9] Instead, there develops a purely objective sales function of commodity aesthetics, objectified in the commodity, which goes beyond the commodity itself. As such, its seed is already contained in simple commodity production, if only by contrast with capitalist development, essen-tially restricted to the body, i.e. the surface of the commodity.

In his novel, *Tui,* Brecht depicts a baker who, as a simple com-modity producer, damaged his sight with eye-strain. 'He earned a lot of money by knowing how to make tiny rolls look appetising. He died, half blind from his strenuous labour, right there in his baking-house, leaving behind a vast fortune.'[10] The objectified illusory solution of the contradiction between use-value and exchange-value shares an origin and function with the active illusory solution provided by sales-talk; but its interference in the sensual relationship of the potential buyer to the commodity is more basic, since it is objective and since, unlike the sales-talk, it can no longer be adequately countered by the buyer.

2 The moulding of the sales assistants

In his novel *Tui,* Brecht mentions the demand from shopkeepers – a demand that had become stronger since the 1920s – for the restyling of their employees, especially the women.

> They demanded that their sales assistants and secretaries be beautiful, and so these women often spent about a third of their salaries on cosmetics. They painted their lips red to make them look healthy and sensual . . . Since they also wore slim high heels, and their behinds protruded, appeared to be consumed by desire for the embraces of the men buying cigars and gloves, or else of their bosses.[11]

The temptation created by those protruding backsides is an aspect of commodity attraction which has been transferred to the salesgirls. The known additional calculation operates thus: since the possessor of money is consumed by desire for something that seems to desire him in return, a further impulse to buy arises. These desires and presentations of the possible are kept on an abstract, general level and cannot be individualized or made concrete.

'Strangely enough', Brecht adds in parenthesis, 'male assistants and chauffeurs were exempted from making up their noses.' Nevertheless, they too were obliged to make themselves look attractive. 'For fear of being withdrawn from the market as unsaleable stock, both ladies *and* gentlemen dye their hair,' Kracauer notes in his survey of employees in 1929. 'People in their forties take up sport to keep slim. *How can I become beautiful?* is the title of a recently published booklet, which, according to advertisements in the press, shows products "that can make one look young and attractive now and for the future." Thus fashion and the economy work hand-in-hand.'[12]

What was emerging at that time, with the mobilization of powerful social fears, especially at office-worker level, mostly among shop assistants of both sexes, was a new standard of looks, behaviour and self-presentation. Kracauer saw in the process a 'selective breeding running its course under the pressure of social relations, which, through the creation of corresponding consumer needs, is necessarily supported by the economy'.

Kracauer sees the content of this process in the fact 'that a type of employee has evolved in Berlin . . . Language, dress, mannerisms and physiognomy become similar, and the result of the process is this uniformly pleasant appearance' which was the prime concern of the personnel department in a well-known Berlin department store. 'We should be like the Americans,' a Department of Employment official told Kracauer. 'A man must put on a friendly face.' The 'craze for numerous beauty parlours . . . the use of cosmetics', and the consulting of 'quacks', has an economic function for employees themselves, especially noticeable when they are unemployed, in improving the saleability of their labour, as that is the only commodity they have to exchange.

In the search for a job 'outward appearances play a decisive role today'. Wrinkles and greying hair lead to 'decreased saleability' of the labour-power commodity. Hence efforts must be made to improve even this commodity's appearance; and the looks and appearance of the capitalist's workforce play the same role for the worker as the commodity's aesthetics do for each commodity-owner.

Kracauer tried to discover 'just what magical powers of appearance' the labour-power commodity needed to offer on the employee-market 'so as to open up the factory gates'. His interpretation of what the required attractive appearance should be is of lasting interest in an analysis of commodity aesthetics, and its influence in the moulding of people. To the question of what he meant by a 'pleasant appearance', the aforementioned personnel manager gave an answer worthy of some consideration: 'Not exactly pretty. The important thing is the morally innocent pink skin colour, you know what I mean.' For Kracauer this combination 'rendered the everyday role played by window displays, office workers and magazines instantly transparent. Its morality should be pink; pink with an undercoat of morality. This is what is wanted by those with the power of selection. They wish to add a coat of varnish to life, to cover up its far-from-rosy reality!' The addition of morality has the function 'of preventing the upsurge of desires. The dismal prospect of naked morality would threaten the existing reality, just as much as a rosy pink which became immorally inflamed with lust. In order to transcend the two, they are bonded together . . . and the further rationalization progresses, the more the morally pink styling takes over.'

The drive to this horrific moulding of a whole social class into a uniform 'pleasantness' is effected primarily through the sales staff, who have to personify the selling function in a commodity–aesthetic manner.[13] The personnel managers of department stores are by no means divorced from the economic world when they act as agents of selective breeding. Their standards of taste, like those of the producers of all commodities with an aesthetic factor, are subject to a perpetual feedback in terms of sales figures. To them the correlation of public taste with the aesthetic stylization of the sales staff's appearance is a factor of immediate consequence for commerce.

Public taste operates here in the same way as the film industry, which is regarded by the agents of film capitalism – according to Brecht's analysis in the *Dreigroschenprozeß* – as 'empirically established' by people whose 'instincts have been sharpened by their material dependence on their analyses being accurate.'[14] The functional cycle that primarily determines the aesthetic standards of those buying labour-power for large stores is that of 'scoring a hit' with the clientele, in the sense of increasing turnover. The function which, in the store's realization of its commodity capital is the appearance of its sales staff, becomes for the latter the sales-function of their labour-power commodity. From here further inroads are made into moulding the appearance and behaviour of the 'huge amorphous unimaginable mass of the public',[15] which was the origin of a previous influence in the form of the sales figures.

But appearances are not the end. To sell, no matter what, must become one's second nature. According to the demands of capital, selling must become an aspect of one's nature, even when it is not in one's own immediate interest. There is a difference between personifying the realization function of one's own or someone else's capital. Actualizing and effectively establishing one's claim depend, not least, on the competition in the labour-power market, as well as on the general competition of retail capital. With a strong position in the labour market, and at the same time strong competition from other capital in the field, retail capital will make absolute demands on its dependent sales assistants.

How can the capitalist convince the seller that he must optimize his turnover? But here, neither objective nor especially egotistical reasons are given. The capitalist can apply leverage in the shape of economic pressure through the threat of salary cuts or redundancy. Due to his powerful position, the capitalist does not need to use the positive aspect of this leverage – the productivity bonus. He may fall back on this only when his position in the labour market becomes weaker, and his seller can easily find another job. When he knows he is in a strong position, because an entire reserve army of sellers is waiting to replace his employees, he will tell himself that it is ineffective to appeal to his sellers for an extra-special effort in his interests. Why should they try too hard to fill someone else's pockets?

Since he understands this, he moves the argument on to a higher level. He develops a cult of selling, becoming the preacher of a pure commercial fanaticism; he never loses sight of his goal – the increase in turnover – which must be internalized by his employees who will not benefit from it, but must nevertheless so deeply absorb it that it takes root in their unconscious. They must become automata of selling, of selling for its own sake. In short, since they are dependent and acting in another's interest, they must implant the sales function in their innermost being. This ideal may lie dormant within capital for a long time if market conditions are unfavourable. Yet it confronts the wage-dependent sales staff ever more harshly as an external coercive force in retail capital, to be administered by its agents as soon as market conditions change into the situation described above.

In Japan, firms suffering severe competition have devised a course of instruction which aims to instil the fanaticism of selling for its own sake.[16] The pressure of competition faced by these companies is heightened by the structure of each sector: they specialize too little, and thus too many firms crowd into the market. In particular, the virtual absence of specialization makes additional demands on the sellers. The programme developed under these conditions is called *Moretsu* (or 'feverishly active'). It involves 'breeding', the goal of which is the fanatical seller whose drives and energy are subordinated to their selling activity. 'The aim is to breed a sales genius, with an elbow of cast-iron, brain like a computer and the constitution of a horse.' In short, 'they want to breed the sales-robot'. The 'breeding' programme starts its day with an hour of strenuous exercises. After breakfast it is time to practise 'self-forgetting'. 'They achieve this by hitting the furniture with clubs and yelling war-cries.' This is succeeded by detailed discussion of the company's sales figures. Whoever is critized by the instructor must literally wallow in the dust while accusing themselves of worthlessness. 'After a time the conviction grows inside the participants on the course that the sales plan must be fulfilled at any cost.'

By hitting the furniture they can work off the aggression which any desire to resist their self-annihilation as the sales function personified may awaken in them. They give themselves courage by arousing their fears. The demons driven out by the ritual of beating and screaming are in fact their own independent impulses. Here a sentence from Brecht's *The Seven Deadly Sins of the Petty Bourgeoisie* can be applied with particularly striking force: 'Whoever wins a victory over themselves also wins the reward.'[17] And the reward here is simply a salary. Whoever has beaten, screamed, and humiliated the demons out of themselves will go about selling as if to drive the commodities out of the store; or rather, drive out the body of the commodity so that its soul, its value, is purified and finally freed from its sinful flesh.

3   The sales location, sales act, and the dissolution of the
    commodity into a form of entertainment; impulse buying
    and the distraction of the public

In the course of a partial socialization of commodity production and distribution, the dynamics of valorization are released to force the constituent moments of the sales act further and further apart, and with their differentiation they become fixed separately and developed in the most profitable arrangement. Presentation and *mise en scène* of the commodities, design of sales location, its architecture, lighting,[18] colours, background noise, and odours; the sales staff, their external appearance and behaviour; the whole business of the sale; each moment in the commodity's metamorphosis, and the environment in which it takes place and which influences it, are all held in the grip of the basic valorization calculation and are functionally adapted towards that end.

All these developments benefit specialized capital, whose profit interest furthers the development. The aesthetics of shops and window displays is the object and means of competition amongst shop-fitters as well as retailers. In this way aesthetic innovation becomes economically indispensible in the field of sales technique which no capitalist trader can afford to ignore. The mechanism does have a tendency increasingly to limit the period of the shops' aesthetic innovation. Thus 'shops are considered outmoded after five to seven years, rather than 20 to 30 years in the old days, and therefore must be completely refurbished.'[19]

The market for shop interior design and sales areas goes on display at a special fair, the 'Euroshop'. 'Many firms who wish to make shops even more modern and attractive', reads the pious report in the trade section of a bourgeois paper (to which one might add 'and those who profit from the competition in the retail sector through their aesthetic of selling'), 'discuss the aspects of shopping experience we need to stimulate in order to increase turnover . . . Ever more sophisticated techniques, and more tasteful designs for the salesroom, are conceived by the shop-fitters.'[20] It is the old story of 'you scratch my back, I'll scratch yours' within capitalism. The shop-fitting capital helps retail capital with a valuable aesthetic weapon for the competitive struggle, the use of which, as it increases in sophistication, becomes compulsory. The shop-fitting capital's advertising conceals a threat: 'If you want to sell, you've got to provide *entertainment.*'[21]

This 'shopping entertainment' offers an additional attraction for buyers, and is thus an armament in the competition between retail capital, which they can no longer do without. 'It was a revelation' the *Frankfurter Allgemeine Zeitung* commented subsequently on the brand new 1967 commodity presentation at Globus, the Zurich department store. The then director, appropriately named Kaufmann [which means salesman or trader], was applying in the new store 'a philosophy of commerce which he later presented again in his fascinating book, *The Key to the Consumer.*'[22]

The commodities are no longer to be displayed in their traditional categories 'but should be arranged thematically to fulfill the needs and dreams of the buyers'. One must not confront the buyer brusquely with a commodity but 'guide them into the "entertainment".' So it can be seen that even the miracle of the transsubstantiation of value from the commodity's use-form into the value-form of money, under the pressure of capital's anxieties, can be turned into a mysterious cult, an initiation ceremony for the buyer lured into acting as the saviour of exchange-value. 'He must not stand aloof,' according to Kaufmann's principles of sales philosophy. 'He must become a participant.' The exhibition of commodities, their inspection, the act of purchase, and all the associated moments, are integrated into the concept of one theatrical total work of art which plays upon the public's willingness to buy. Thus the salesroom is designed as a stage, purpose-built to convey entertainment to its audience that will stimulate a heightened desire to spend. 'On this stage the sale is initiated. This stage is the most important element in sales promotion.'

This aesthetic innovation of the salesroom into a 'stage for entertainment' on which a variety of commodities are arranged to reflect the audience's dreams, to overcome their reservations, and provoke a purchase, was a pioneering exercise at a time marked by a general change in the selling trend. 'Fashion, in the meantime, had developed into a totality which affected the individual's whole appearance. A new dress required new stockings and shoes in a matching colour-scheme, a suitable handbag and new make-up. Fashion, even spread beyond clothing, affecting other areas such as house interiors.' Boutiques led the way in conquering this market, 'mushrooming ever since', probably because their profits were well above the average in the retail trade.

In this situation,[23] it was the department stores in particular which had to keep up with what was euphemistically and naively termed 'a rising standard of living'. Kaufmann's innovation was immediately demonstrated to be a pioneering breakthrough. 'The entertainment-stage at the Globus department store became a mecca to which retailers from all over the world made an annual pilgrimage.' There they hoped to gain access to their Holy of Holies, to receive newly disclosed their driving force and determining aim.

The outcome was that, to turn a proverb on its head, the early bird lost his worm. Kaufmann was obliged to resign because 'the entertainment programme at Globus did not fulfill expectations.' The turnover per employee in 1970 was only 29,000 Swiss Francs, while department stores in the Federal Republic had figures of between DM70,000 and DM84,000 per worker. Kaufmann's successor, Calveti, pragmatically reduced the task. 'Entertainment shopping' in his revised formula, 'has to be initiated by the commodity and not from the stage.'

However, the 'Seven Worlds of Globus' are already undergoing a resurrection in the new Wertheim store in West Berlin's Kurfürstendamm.

> In a row of elegantly furnished shops and boutiques, groups of commodities which fulfill the most sophisticated of needs are arranged. Among other things, customers can find a 'Trend Shop, Fifth Avenue', a Western shop, 'Chisolm Trail, Santa Fé', and a beauty salon, 'Madame'. Fashionable footwear is for sale at 'Boots Inn', and the latest records at 'Blues Inn.'[24]

The language of capital draws greatly on Wall Street even when the valorization standpoint is persuasively denied. Those who are to be fooled must pay for their entertainment. The management calculates that the new store will be one 'which, despite offering the full range of everyday products, is consciously aimed at the more sophisticated market (fashionable brand-name goods). Moreover, Wertheim, like the other stores, prefers a younger clientele in the high income bracket.'[25]

In contrast to the strategy of 'entertainment shopping', it appears that the 'purchasing strategy' is hardly perceived as such. From the standpoint of exchange-value and on a higher level, from the standpoint of valorization, it would be ideal if the monied class could be made to buy 'without reflecting on the necessity of an acquisition',[26] as suggested by the soul of capital in a bourgeois newspaper's financial section. In pursuit of this ideal, in so far as it is achieveable, capital and its applied science of consumer research have invented the term 'impulse buying'. In order to induce it, styling, display and pricing of the commodity are assigned specific tasks. It is intended for a surprise encounter with the distracted customer. The commodity put on view is not displayed as the main article one is looking for, but appears as a seemingly incidental commodity. For example, the shoe firm Wosana achieved 'the highest growth rate (in 1971 around 100 per cent) . . . by distributing through food stores and supermarkets as well as drugstores and perfumeries (around 20 per cent growth).'[27]

The prices are consciously calculated to attract 'impulse buying' by ensuring that they retail at under DM20. The styling displays the commodity as if it had already been bought. 'Accordingly, some Wosana products are offered in clear plastic with a handle.' Viewing the merchandise through the wrapping replaces any physical contact or testing of the commodity which acts as a synthetic reminder that the actual test for use-value has been made to seem superfluous. The handle is already familiar from the carrier bags in which one carries away one's commodities. Everything is arranged so as not to inconvenience, since every pause in the act of buying can provide a break-off point, allowing time for reflection on the necessity of what one is actually acquiring. The purchase, being hardly recognized as such, and therefore unconsidered, also depends like 'entertainment shopping' on an element of distraction. If the unconsidered purchase happens, literally by chance on the sidelines, the development of 'entertainment shopping' itself places the incidental at the centre of its aesthetic efforts at representing commodity capital, thus operating as an entertaining distraction for the public.

In the 1970 Euroshop fair in Düsseldorf this new style of selling appeared on the horizon to establish a general standard. 'One can expect,' reported the biggest shopfitters in the Federal Republic, 'that the activation of the sales process will culminate in an increasingly strong attempt to combine supply with entertainment.'[28] With entertainment, or amusement, an additional vehicle for aesthetic commodity attraction arrives on the salesroom's 'entertainment' stage.[29] This involves new functions for the sales agents. At the fair it was said that 'the retailer of the future must be both shopkeeper and impresario rolled into one.'[30] As an experiment, some department stores changed the emphasis of their advertising. 'Relax with us,' proposed a West Berlin concern in the autumn of 1971, 'in the fascinating world of a large department store. Where you can buy a lot of fun for very little money. And without cash! Simply use your Gold Card. We wish you an enjoyable time shopping at *XYZ*.'[31]

These performances, an extra means of seduction evolved from the commodity, still have to be paid for by the buyers. The thinking behind the 'amusement store' remains the same as in the 'entertainment stage', i.e. takings per employee and profit on turnover. Here the borderline between the commodity and the sales process begins to blur, as already happened long before between use-value and commodity aesthetics. Now, when a commodity is sold, the customer not only pays for its styling and the name made famous through advertising, but also for the styling of the selling process. As far as the commodity is concerned, conscious efforts are made to shift the emphasis from the specific commodity to the experience of consumption.

Ultimately the aestheticization of commodities means that they tend to dissolve into enjoyable experiences, or into the appearance of those experiences, detached from the commodity itself. The tendency to sell these processes as material/immaterial types of commodities leaves no time to consider their use-value. By selling the commodity in the form of absolute consumption, the market remains unsatiated.

To establish this trend, it is not enough to mould and remould the army of sellers; one must condition the instincts and behaviour of the 'public at large'. And since young people are easiest to manipulate, they become the instrument and expression of a general trend towards moulding. Their fetishization is both expression and instrument in one. We can now investigate the mechanics of this relation with the aid of examples.

4   The moulding of the world of buyers: clothes as
    packaging; the language of love; cosmetics; the
    neutralizing and reprogramming of body odour

Advertising transfers its breadth of experience and calculation to its target groups. It treats its human targets like commodities, to whom it offers the solution to their problem of realization. Clothes are advertised like packaging as a means of sales promotion. This is one of the many ways in which commodity aesthetics takes possession of people.

The two central areas in which advertising offers, by means of commodities, to solve the problems of 'scoring hits' and sales are, on the one hand, following a career of the labour market and, on the other, gaining the respect of and attracting others. 'How is it that clever and competent people don't make it in their careers?' was the question put by a wool advertisement in 1968. 'Don't call it bad luck if it is only a matter of "packaging". You can sell yourself better in a new suit! And that is often what counts in life.'[32] A woman whose romance has failed and who is looking for a new partner was recommended by *Twen* magazine in 1969, as 'step 9' in its advice, to 'become overwhelmingly pretty . . . Why not try what you've never tried before? If you want to scour the market, you've got to show yourself in your best packaging.'[33] Where love succeeds, brought about by this fashionable packaging, and leads to encounters which under existing conditions appear in the form of a commodity–cash nexus, the cost of clothes can be interpreted as 'capital investment'.

This is the term with which the managing direct of the Frankfurt boutique chain, *Elfi*, sums up the attitudes of his female clientele: according to the *Frankfurter Rundschau*; Horst Weiß is reported 'to have been soberly observing for years the trade in dresses, blouses, skirts, woollens, coats, jackets and trousers'.[34] His eyes have put themselves at the service of retail capital, of which he is the personification, and in their own sober way, they see only sheer valorization. His female customers appear to this 'personification of capital' to be buying packages to sell themselves in. He sees his own function as the provider of these packages. 'Office girls and shop assistants', Weiß comments on his female customers, 'invest all their money in fashion, not only to be chic . . . but also in the hope of an eventual return on their investment. Given the choice either of buying clothes or of eating regularly for the rest of the month, they go for the dress in the hope that their new outfit will attract someone who will invite them out for a meal.'[35]

When *Twen* spoke of offering 'your best packaging' when a woman is looking for a man, this turn of phrase may betray conscious or open cynicism, since the most desirable part of this technique is the package itself, which acts as a functionally determined beautiful illusion. When the calculation of this functional determination works it surpasses all others, and a new standard of achievement in one's career or love-life can be established. The driving force, however, was not the setting up of this new standard, which was only a means or a side-effect of the standpoint of determining instinctual drives and interests.

These successful ploys in the pursuit of love and achievement are, with this turnaround, only a by-product of the determined strategies of the profit motive; for these strategies are intended to commercialize certain commodities out of the complex of use-values involved in careers and romance. Their tactic is to offer the appropriate commodities to customers as a means of selling themselves. Essentially it involves promoting people's willingness to purchase, which cannot be detached from the purpose and technique of the general saleability of people. From the standpoint of the firm which advertises, the essential goal is the valorization of its capital, but an intermediate and lasting result is the specific moulding of behavioural and emotional patterns. For instance, the Dutch firm, De Beers, presently active in the Federal Republic, is busily engaged in profiting from having effected a change in the language of love; that is, the way in which lovers assure each other of their affection. To be precise, it seeks 'to establish the diamond' as a 'symbol of love' in Germany and thus to open up a whole new stratum of buyers. [36] De Beers 'is not without success' already, and 'will continue this year with a new campaign in the DM200–1,000 price range in order to reach a wider section of the public'. Soon millions of women can expect as an expression of their suitors' love 'at the very least' a diamond engagement ring, and perhaps necklace and earrings as a wedding gift. [37]

The company that creates these expectations is not just plugging a gap in the market, for the campaign contains a snag for the ordinary people it is directed at. The slogan 'Diamonds are for love', 'will have to console quite a few people', as the publication *Blick durch die Wirtschaft*, which is used to such claims, commented coolly. 'Many who put a valuable diamond ring on their wives' fingers expect not only a tender "thank you", but also a considerable appreciation of their investment. But, just as many a love diminishes with the years, the value of the "symbols of love" could depreciate. At least this is what the international market in precious stones expects.' [38] As businessmen they cannot but respect De Beers Consolidated Mines Ltd., since they are a world leader. Large diamonds, which few can afford, are indeed expected to rise in value, but the smaller ones, with which De Beers tries to 'satisfy' the small buyer, are not only expected to depreciate, and thus meet a declining demand from value-conscious investors, [39] but they 'are becoming more numerous as a by-product of industrially cut diamonds'. [40] Thus De Beers is not only exploiting a gap in the market, but is also swiftly unloading vast amounts of a depreciating commodity onto the market, with a huge propaganda exercise as a 'symbol of love' for the small man.

If one branch of capitalism commercializes the packaging of humans, and another their love tokens, a third caters for the actual physical appearance, the way their skin feels and smells, their make-up, and the colour, sheen and cut of their hair. The make-up of the female face is the concern of agents called 'visagistes'. 'What kind of face is today's woman wearing in the winter of 1971-2?', begins a report by a fashion correspondent for *Frankfurter Rundschau.* 'Visagistes are no longer going for a natural look but, on the contrary, extreme artificiality. The cosmetics industry is keen to sell women as many products as possible. Hubbart Ayer alone recommends 13 for a single make-up image and promises – the promise of use-value – to turn every Cinderella into a fairytale Princess.'[41]

The services the cosmetics' industry offers women bear a macabre functional resemblance in their promise of use-value to those that advertising agencies provide for capital. In both cases it is a matter of promoting a style, with the difference that individual customers are buying both the styling commodities and their own saleability. So Cinderella vanishes into the Princess packaging which, without the lovely illusion provided by capital, cannot survive alone as appearance and shrivels to a pitiful remnant. Whoever learns that the Princess's features contain the function and character of packaging will hardly be enamoured of her. Yet this is how she is supposed to look, according to the dictates of the Paris visagistes:

> Three pastel shades shimmer round the eye. The inside of the lips a pink-beige, the outside super-brilliant a blue-beige. Added to this, coyly rounded apple cheeks are created . . . Stars and hearts make novel beauty spots at the corner of the eye or on the chin. Eyebrows are heavily plucked and even earlobes get a dash of colour. Geometrical shapes, quadrants and triangles, are painted on in Rubinstein's tawny-gold compact powder. Lips at Helena Rubinstein are copper-beige and brown-gold, eyelashes are slightly ruffled, the eyes large as if astonished, with slightly-angled eyebrows.[42]

The doubly determined traits of commodity aesthetics, as moments in the aesthetics of cosmetic commodities as well as of the self-advertising styling of the human commodity, contain an awful role reversal. If the functional determination of these traits is recognized at once, the pathetically calculated routine, out of the individual's control, becomes apparent in those coy cheeks, and behind the astonished eyes one can sense monotony and boredom. The goddess-packaging serves as a glittering straitjacket, a glossy recompense for subjection and degradation to a second-rate existence. Furthermore, maintaining the packaging is not only expensive but it keeps one occupied. The significance of the strain of keeping up the image lies in the drain on social time taken by countless women to manufacture their appearance.

By gaining this new face one simultaneously loses one's own. The body shares a similar fate; the commercialization of its surface appearance does not leave the sensual being unaffected. When capital chooses to profit from bodycare, there is no way that the existing relationship of the individual to their body can withstand this avaricious power.

The 10 per cent rise in cosmetic commodities' turnover between 1966 and 1967 in the Federal Republic to over three billion Deutschmarks 'made the beauty industry almost the only expanding branch of the German economy' during the recession.[43] The 1967 advertising budget for some 130 firms was about DM175 million, and surpassed both budgets for cars and spirits; it was only exceeded by washing powders and detergents. With decreasing returns and dwindling investment opportunities, capital has moved into the 'beauty industry'. With as much force as its hunger for profits pushed to expand the cosmetics market, these strategies penetrated the pores of human sensuality. Once the recession was over, the boom accelerated.[44] This sector managed to expand further and increased profit rates by a massive propaganda campaign with the purely instrumental aim of subjecting the individual's relationship to their own and others' bodies to a fundamental revolution. Wherever insecurity, fear, or unsatisfied urges could be assuaged with cosmetic commodities, advertising applied the pressure.

Women have been the traditional market for the industry, its largest sector being that of haircare.[45] The expansion introduced new commodities,[46] or at least new stylings, combined with new marketing strategies. A striking example is the introduction of 'intimate deodorants' and other defences against one's own body smells. A saturation campaign managed to radicalize and spread socially an idiosyncratic prejudice against smells, notably sexually stimulating ones. An intermediate report in 1968 shows its striking success, increasing specifically among adolescents, once again the 'ideal customers': protections against their own body odour were used by 43 per cent of females between 16 and 60, and already 87 per cent of 19-year-olds were using such products.[47] It is essential to note the specific effect of such items on human sensuality. The threshold of stimulation is lowered by their use, since the forbidden odours will register much more strongly. Where these smells still linger, or return, the perception of them is now undeniable and idiosyncratically established. From now on the human body smells repellant. Anxiety-ridden nausea bringing feelings of revulsion leads to panicky defensiveness and evasion and the idiosyncracy thus engineered tends to become aggressive. Thus a new social norm of hygiene is established, anchored powerfully and directly as a norm in the individual's senses, and completely opposed to what is considered dirty and repugnant. This process can be called the moulding of sensuality. It demonstrates vividly how blind mechanisms of profit-making, as an essentially indifferent means to an end and a by-product of profit, can alter human sensuality.

Since women have in principle been conquered by cosmetics, the industry's expansion will depend on new products, as well as the mass-marketing of luxury goods previously available only to the élite. During the reorganization of the Helena Rubinstein company from 1965 onwards, 'one had to fight against the tendency to only offer something to the elegant mature woman.'[48] That is, one had to broach the mass-market.

Cosmetics as mass commodities was the market strategy of the Pond organization. 'The company is not addressing itself to the "lady of leisure", who already regularly buys a variety of products for face and bodycare, but to the majority of the female population who, as "average customers", regard the range of cosmetics as too complicated and expensive.' In pursuit of this market expansion, traditional stereotypes of the female image are rephrased, reinforced, and interwoven with its sales programme. '"Health and beauty means happiness" is the formula to which market researchers have reduced the conceptual universe for the majority of women.' Thus reads a completely uncritical report in the trade columns of a bourgeois newspaper.[49] The starting-point is the housewife's frustrations. 'They lack the appreciation and sense of achievement that career women get,' and this is what the firm wishes to remedy with its creams and lotions. The advertising identifies particular frustrations, and stalks its 'target group, which is roughly 80 per cent of the female population', with its slogan 'Health and beauty means happiness', once again the instrument and by-product of a profit-strategy. This is how capital homes in on fears and unsatisfied longings, redirecting attention, and defining the body in a new way, both its look, and its smell, as well as its tactile sense and self-perception.

5   The moulding of men – men's toiletries; clean clothes
    every day; the image of masculinity; the penis enters the
    commodity arena

One line of attack by the cosmetics industry is suggested by the fact that in 1967 'the amount spent on advertising men's perfumes was seven times that on ladies.'[50] Capital interested in turning men on to cosmetics had to start from the assumption that, in this area, particularly strong, traditionally deep-rooted, inhibitions had to be overcome. Many men shied away from using cosmetics 'for fear of being considered homosexual, or effeminate.'[51] The disproportionate use of advertising can thus be explained by the fact that, despite the prejudices that advertising had to overcome, capital noticed a huge gap in the marketing of men's relationship to their bodies. The market research institute, 'Contest', prophesied an 'immense willingness to use cosmetics even among men.' Marplan opinion polls had shown the way to exploit narcissism, particularly amongst adolescents and young men. Older men were again reminded of the huge anxieties they could face if they did not follow the new standards of youthful masculinity. The 'addiction to youth in our culture' acts on older men as a powerful compulsion towards 'cosmetic behaviour'.

Even the Rubinstein organization, from its New York headquarters, had been trying since 1965 to open up new markets.

'A special programme for black customers was developed, and for overseas markets, men's toiletries were added.'[52]

In the overall market for male cosmetics, it is still mainly shaving and hair lotions that do the biggest business. A common factor is that their advertising, especially of hair preparations, is associated with a pseudo-medical rationalization which helps to overcome the masculine inhibitions and fears of appearing effeminate. This rationalization, aided by such terms as 'healthy' and 'clean', is certain to influence the development of 'cosmetic behaviour' among men in the Federal Republic. It is probably through the pseudo-hygiene of suppressing body odours that capital will reach the immediate masculine cosmetics sector of the market.

In the menswear market, it is at present the uniformity of aesthetic innovation and the laborious way human beings have been transformed which particularly catches the eye, since this sector has been up till now relatively stable: changes in fashion occurred on a much smaller scale than for women. The interest in generally effective aesthetic innovation, i.e. in outdating clothes in current use, joined forces with the interests of large-scale capital to monopolize certain sectors of the market, creating new concepts in which marketing and fashion were fully amalgamated. Through the totalization of design, the distinctions between individual commodities became blurred to make way for entire commodity-complexes. One purchase was intended to trigger many others, and this strategy, successfully tested on women, is now being introduced on the menswear market.

The first to use this strategy were the boutiques. Now one sees the arrival of the franchise system which has opened up self-contained boutiques inside still nominally independent menswear shops. A contract of cooperation was recenty agreed between one of the Federal Republic's largest wholesale textile buyers, Sütex,[53] and Atomic Fashions,[54] an outlet for one of the country's biggest textile manufacturers, which may serve to illustrate this principle of marketing. One might infer from its name that the 'Atomic Idea' is destined to devastate the market. But on the contrary the conception seeks to move away from the elemental commodity towards a fashionably integrated combined-commodity molecule. Equally, this leads away from the disjunction of independent retailers towards the setting up of a powerful uniform distribution network.

The Atomic Idea is at its nucleus a franchise system in which independent retailers sign a contract with Atomic Fashions, which entitles them to supply and sell a range of commodities and services for men, subject to certain rules of shop design, price range, and styling. With this package come complete shops, Atomic Men's Centres, and departments, Atomic Men's Depots.[55]

The advertising and 'brand promotion' are directed from Atomic Fashions' headquarters, which also decides everything to do with styling and which will make these shops uniformly recognizable, so that the commodities inside are simply a dependent accessory, a mere atom in the macro-molecule of the image. This image, in which the individual commodity is but a transitory moment, must assimilate the customer to itself. Whoever takes the first step must groom and supplement their own image within this system. They become the ideal customers in an aesthetic use-value monopoly, who have to respond to all the details of fashionable innovation as well as its ever-changing trends. They are on their way to becoming 'commodity subscribers'. However, the firm in whose distribution network they have been caught not only creates the image of the shops under its control and of the complex of commodities they stock, but it also keeps a grip on the image of the clientele.

The changes in market structure of the isolated example outlined above unleash powerful forces which, in pursuit of profit, manipulate the sensuality of the targeted group. It is not possible to describe the entire context of this process within the scale of this book. So for our purposes it must suffice to prove that, and demonstrate how this process, termed 'sensuality moulding', turns the sensual being – in this case men – into a dependent variable of the capital valorization process. For this purpose we shall give relatively random phenomenon as samples for analysis.

In late 1969, capitalist industry announced a 'new trend in pullovers'.[56] Part of this campaign, the other side of aesthetic innovation, was dedicated to out-dating the pullovers currently being worn. 'There are plenty of boring jumpers. We've had enough! Now super-long jumpers with belts are in fashion.' Which basically means stopping whatever is in use and bringing in the new. The ideal, to which this type of propaganda approximates, would be a commanding voice in which orders are given, forbidding the further usage of existing use-values. But such commands would be unprofitable, for why should they be obeyed? Propaganda for fashionable innovation is only effective if it influences the sensual being by playing on its desires and fears. In the case in point, capital campaigns for a new fashion in pullovers, since that is where its interest lies, by proclaiming a new definition of secondary male sexual characteristics, which is what the potential buyers want, and which is also the bait by which capital hooks them. 'The emphasis is again on the chest (the more physical, the more fashionable). Chunky ribs and strong colours stress the fact that we're men.' And the one who decides this is the 'eunuch of industry' – capital.[57]

It is apparent that this eunuch is also keen to turn his attention to the appearance of masculinity below the belt. Worn loosely over the skintight pullover, the belt serves no real purpose and functions only as a cosmetic appearance. Being worn casually, it seems to emphasize lasciviously the wearer's slimness, that fetishistic attribute of youth. Or, being a leather thong, it may 'signify' a symbolic object of libidinal fixation, a luxurious sense of power for its own sake.[58]

Under the heading 'The new jumpers have arrived!' the same firm advertised, two years later, appealing to people with a specific fetishistic disposition through the seductive command, 'Fall in for the new military look'.[59] From the standpoint of the company advertising, obviously its only concern is the sale of its commodities, but in order to sell them the current image of masculinity has first to be reviewed.

In search of new investment and high profit, capital even had its nose into the extra-long jumper. The market for men's underwear was until recently traditionally much narrower than for women, because the latter wash and change their briefs more often and thus wear them out and also, because of women's passive sexual role in a patriarchal society, their underwear has taken on seductive implications. On the underwear market, women were thus ideal customers. In other words, the ideal customer for underwear-capital has 'feminine traits'. But for the purposes of expanding the male market in such clothes, these traits had to be instilled into the buying masses, and thus their sensual being and conception of themselves as men had to be adjusted accordingly. This manipulation would work on the one hand on considerations of hygiene, and on the other hand on narcissistic male fantasies through the deployment of sexual features.

In 1970 a group making men's underwear tried to publicize the idea of a daily change of underwear. Not without an element of humour the group advertised its claim to have developed special underwear specifically suited to daily changing. In fact they had merely created a new trademark, consisting of a symbol and brand name, which they attached to a sector of their output.

As evidence of this we can analyse two advertisements in *Der Spiegel*.[60] The two cross-refer, the second appearing in the magazine two pages after the first. The first is in monochrome, and the second coloured yellow, sky-blue, and pale-green. The first shows a photo of nine men, beer glasses in hand, standing in a bar. Seven are wearing masks of pigs' heads, while two show likeable human faces. The caption reads, 'Only 10 per cent of men change their underwear daily'. The reader, of course, gets the message that the others are pigs. If someone is found not to change daily, he will lose his human face. The second advertisement shows the clean, bright world of Sympa Fresh-wear, 'specially designed for daily changing'. Whether as a joke or an insult the copy continues: 'Now their wives have it easier' – Since they have to do the laundry more often? – 'Since they can ensure that their men never have to do without the comfortable feel of fresh underwear.'

The firm's strategy defines the group who already change their underwear daily as a sub-market, although the seeming accuracy of 10 per cent may be arbitrary and probably too high. The new brand tends to create a monopoly in this sub-market, and the establishment of a monopoly, based on an illusion, at the same time helps to broaden this captured sub-market. He who chooses not to change his underwear daily, have it washed, and thus does not fulfill the dreams of the washing-powder industry, is liable to be branded a filthy pig. Thus this marketing ploy helps to set a new standard in men's relationship with their bodies. The standard is not entirely new but, in conjunction with existing standards, it forces a hygiene-tendency, which exploits insecurity or guilt-feelings about the body. In effect the profit motive of capital has pushed affect-moulding towards an increased distancing from the body itself, and the means of estrangement and repression is the advertised commodity. The extent to which the repression is ultimately shut away behind a wall of nausea reinforces human dependence on the commodity. The sensual being, however, has been remoulded. Incidental elements, sometimes a hindrance, but also moments of greatest pleasure, have now been condemned and turned into a barrier against pleasure in both senses. Without it, pleasure is assaulted and vitiated: where it lingers, it disables the capacity for pleasure, arousing fear and repugnance.

The second approach to breeding the ideal customer for underwear lies in the direction of sexy underwear for men. Passing through those 'ideal customers' – the young – the path leads towards influencing older generations through propaganda for youthfulness. Their attributes are the advertised commodities themselves, their advertising designed for more than just the sale of an isolated commodity. What is being thrust on the public is a whole complex of sexual perception, appearance, and experience. Since capital producing underpants is aiming for a niche in a profitable market, underpants are necessarily in the spotlight. Since they must be saleable at monopoly prices, they must be shown in the right light, and thus, once again, the body is emphasized. As in the case of suits, their saleability is highlighted by the quality of the packaging. Packages are advertised in a way which stresses the improvement in sales due to advantageous presentation. The advertised underpants are made into a 'hit' by underlining the fact that they make the body a 'hit'. They become the body's snug marketing package, and thus the concerns of capital appear, as it were, in underwear and, by seeming to take an interest in the body, promote commodities by suggesting that they advertise the body itself.

The body, on whose behalf all this advertising is happening, adopts the compulsory traits of a brand-named product; in the same way, it is not the body itself but the effective advertising image which is being promoted. Capital's interest in the body even contains certain aspects which are rather more detrimental to it than the Christian aversion to the flesh, which capital propagates as its missionary in a different constellation. Not only does men's image change (although there is nothing wrong with a conscious change, which men perhaps need), but men are now obliged to maintain a certain image as an attribute of their masculinity which, apart from the effort involved in cultivating the appearance, requires the continuous acquisition of a growing number of commodities. Once again, people share the same fate as commodities. Each one is supposed to behave like a cheap and powerless carbon-copy of a brand-named commodity manufacturer; and each must market themselves as a brand article.

Within this context of the brand image, the male member and other attributes enter the arena, propelled by the underwear manufacturer's profit interest. The purchase of underwear is provoked by emphasizing the penis.[61] Thus, after centuries of increasing prohibition, the penis is on public show again as part of an image.[62] The garments that display it have become multi-coloured, as their promise of use-value involves advertising the body. But their promises operate on a different level from what the body can fulfill. The redemption adequate to the promises would be the perception that stays with them through all the advertising. Although the purchase of these commodities is motivated by a desire for sexual intercourse, they appear designed merely for admiration in the mirror. To use Sartre's terminology, it is being-for-others that they promise by way of merely being-for-oneself. Thus it is a question of illusion-for-others.

Nowadays, adolescent males are offered a commodity which, by exaggeration of a trend, throws light on this trend. These are underpants which equip the wearer with a phallic façade. Under the brand name 'Mother wouldn't like it', they are on sale to English adolescents as underpants that 'awaken the beast in you'.[63] An advertising illustration shows the slim, hairless bodies of two youths from neck to knees. They wear briefs as tight as bikini bottoms, narrowly restricting the animal secret they promise in their package. Incidentally, they have no slit for urination, not being intended as practical underpants but only as a costume for exhibition. The joke is that they have animal heads printed over the penis. The effect is supposed to trigger a purchase, but what are they promising? The suggestion is, surely, that whoever buys them will be endowed with the promise of menacing phallic masculinity and animal potency.

Considering more closely the context of the commodity's promise of use-value alongside the consumer's needs, one discovers one of the rules of the game, the basic *quid pro quo* of commodity aesthetics, which shows how, when an object is focused upon by commodity aesthetics, the consumer's needs can disappear into obscurity. What makes the customer buy may be the wish, articulated in the commodity as 'Mother wouldn't like it', to win acknowledgement as a phallic hero. Freud has shown how a child's dreams of potency are shattered time and again by many experiences of his organ's inadequacy. The dissolution of the Oedipus complex does not presuppose an actual encounter with the rival father's threat of castration; instead the complex is dissolved by this sense of inadequacy, not all at once but in a long chain of interlinked, repeated and painful frustrations. If the adolescent is lured by its promise into buying the commodity to gain acceptance as a phallic hero, he buys not merely to be packaged as one, but actually to *be* one. The commodity's illusion promises its *being*. However, the bought commodity only endows him with the illusion of what he desires. At best it serves merely as an imaginary satisfaction of omnipotent phallic fantasies such as those exploited by comic strips. The commodity then, can only serve as a prop for heroic fantasies.

But the matter does not end there. After the commodity has brought psycho-sexual emotions to the surface, offering itself as an aid to phallic fantasy, its electrifying emptiness tends to create imaginary spaces in reality. What has been brought to light cannot exist on its own, but the forms of interaction that develop around such props remain wildly imaginary. A representative example of other props is the underpants that 'awaken the beast in you'. They are packages bought because they promise more than they can deliver; they may not be opened, because the contents have to hide shamefacedly behind the over-suggestive surface. Yet the latter fulfills its function by indicating the nature of the contents, while at the same time signifying that it is merely flimsy packaging. The ultimate package, which would agree with Oscar Wilde, that 'It's only shallow people who do not judge by appearances,'[64] by admitting to be no more than a showy front with nothing behind it, would have played its last card and be torn to pieces in a mixture of angry frustration, scorn and relief. Wherever it is worn, the fascinating package creates imaginary spaces, within which relationships develop, of the sort which had induced the customer to buy.

Since advertising for such commodities is, in effect, merely advertising for advertising, the chain of *quid pro quo* is unbroken by the purchase. By wearing these packages, the advertising continues. Whoever bought in order to appear desirable, is betrayed once more by the commodity. For it only endows the buyer with an advertisement as non-specific and generalized as its own message, since advertising, within the framework of the market, addresses itself to the wide world of anyone with money.

Without discrimination, commodity aesthetics smiles invitingly on everyone, the soul of the commodity being as ingratiating as it is promiscuous. To stimulate desire in every possible way as commodity aesthetics does indiscriminately, 'by prostituting [the] body to the lust of another',[65] as the commodity does, can only make sense from the standpoint of exchange-value. Whoever buys such commodities, which in effect advertise the body, prostitutes their appearance, packages their sexual attributes into something that can be bought, and offers them to anyone who merely looks at them.

Andy Warhol designed a record sleeve for a US company which transfers the advertisement for the penis back on to the surface of another commodity, the disc. The retailers were supplied with appropriate dummies for display, and the album sold in great numbers, to the great benefit of the company whose newly founded subsidiary in the Federal Republic quickly established itself, 'not without help from this album.'[66] The cover shows skintight small-hipped jeans from the belt down to the upper thighs. The snugly-fitting material reveals every contour of the body. Emphasized by Warhol's technique of touching up the photograph, the penis is extremely clearly outlined. A real zip, which can be opened, is inserted into the cover.[67]

Whoever buys the record, purchases along with it a copy of a young man's fly, the package identified by the graphic trick which stresses the penis and highly stylizes the promised content. The buyer acquires the possibility of opening the package, and the zip and finds . . . nothing. It is a reversal of the tale of the Emperor's new clothes: the tale of the buyers' new bodies. They buy only packages which seem to be more than they are. Warhol may present himself as an enlightened critic of society, with his earlier signed replicas of soupcans, which make a point by apparently accepting the dominant fraudulence in society and pushing it to the limit, so that even the most stupid can see what lies behind the advertisements.

Perhaps he goes even further and intends the penis joke on the sleeve to suggest liberation from the false magic of the commodity aesthetics which are imposed on people. The implication of the joke would be that wherever there are invitations one should accept them: each promising opportunity should be grasped, and where a package glamorously offers a real content, unwrap it. Such behaviour could scare off the 'foul magic of the commodity' (W. Benjamin) and reduce the imaginatively supercharged objects to their natural level.

If Warhol had hinted at this or some equally enlightened message in his product, we could criticize more than just the way this supposed intervention is conveyed. Not only does he unmask commodity aesthetics in a way which allows its mask to become an even more sophisticated advertisement than that which was removed; but even worse, commodity aesthetics, given a dose of its own medicine, inculcates a cynicism linked with the frustration that all one gets one's hands on is mere packaging. On being opened, however, and found to be empty, the package does not withdraw its imaginary space, with its tempting illusions and behavioural inhibitions. Rather, the unmasked void appears to rebound on the purchaser, leaving him ashamed and addicted. If this is so, Warhol's commodity package of enlightenment and frustration does not arouse anger or make any relationships apparent. In a curious way this unsatisfiable desire seems to lead merely to acquiescence, for its own sake as it achieves no reward for acquiescing, which is in no way a relationship of true pleasure.

6   Trends in the moulding of sensuality: the social genesis
    of compulsory rejuvenation; uses of the youth image; the
    world of interiors as a sexual landscape in which no one
    ages, yet many die

In the late 1920s Kracauer noticed that ageing employees were treated worse than even the most ruthless valorization standpoint warranted. He set this in the context of a 'nowadays general abandonment of the old', and continues: 'Not only the workforce but the whole nation has turned away from them, and idolises youth to a disconcerting extent. It is a fetish for all magazines and their readers to court the custom of the old with rejuvenating potions.' The old pursue the young as if mesmerized, 'although it would be a grave error to consider the young to be life itself.'[68] For the young are subject to a law that Brecht formulated a few years later as the essence of the *Seven Deadly Sins of the Petty Bourgeoisie*, namely 'Beauty will perish and youth pass away!'[69]

The elderly, with the social rank and privilege they have achieved thanks to a wasted youth, feel useless and long for the old days. Kracauer hints at the cause of this empty and misdirected life-cycle rather cautiously, either for reasons of camouflage, or else due to his humanistic but contemplative and pacifist tradition, which leads him to interpret 'this idolatry of the young' partly as a reflex of capitalist economics, and partly as a reaction to specific changes in the spheres of production and administration.

There was no doubt that 'rationalized production methods favoured this misunderstanding, if they were not themselves the cause of it.' This push towards rationalization which revolutionized production and administration in the 1920's, along with technological innovation, made new demands on, in particular, employees' professional qualifications. These demands could be met naturally by the younger generation since their education coincided with these changes. It also meant a greater degree of exploitation, without retraining programmes or job relocation schemes, for the older generation of employees. It was a catastrophe for millions; being over 30 became a curse. The outlook for many seemed as dark as that of the unemployed clerk who replied on a trade-union questionnaire: '"The future is bleak and hopeless. An early death would be best" – This was written by a 32-year-old, married with two children.'[70] Such experiences suffered by millions served to place a high value across the whole of society on youth, whose glamour is enhanced by the secret fears of being aged under capitalism. However, youth worship and the consequent displacement of the old has an extra implication which cannot be explained even by the inhuman rationality of capitalist exploitation.

Kracauer interprets this implication as a reflex of the meaninglessness of life in the capitalist world, in as far as this reflex action is determined by its functions. But he only hints at this vaguely.

Since the rationalized economy is unsure of its own meaning, it 'prohibits' the working masses from questioning the meaning of their existence.

> But if people are not allowed to look forward to a meaningful end, even the ultimate end, their death, will slip from their grasp. Their life, which should be contrasted with death, in order to be a life at all, is obstructed and drifts back to its origins, their youth. Their origins become a perverted fulfilment since the genuine one is made impossible. The dominant mode of business cannot be analysed successfully, so sheer vitality triumphs.[71]

The capital valorization into which they are shackled has no meaning for the wage-dependent masses; their lives are determined by the valorization functions of capitalism, but this is meaningless in itself – mere wage-slavery, a means of making a living, which is controlled, under this economic system, not by life's real needs, but solely by the achievement of surpluses and profits. To live and toil as a worker under capitalism offers no achievement upon which people can look back fulfilled, unlike under socialism, where everybody has a share in each machine, factory, or housing estate he or she has helped to build. Always working for others ultimately means working for nothing at all. This experience becomes inexorable with the approach of ageing and death, for, if the contradictions of class relations are not made apparent, and without a class-based organization, the experience of being old recurs and seems even harder to bear. Only unenlightened, not class-conscious, expectations drift back to 'youth'.

Youth appeal is put to many uses by commodity aesthetics. From the world of commodities it radiates back to the public and reinforces a moulding of sensuality which takes youthfulness as its model. The origin and effect of this moulding are personified by female sales assistants. Their youthfulness is seized upon by capital as a selling function, while the 'old' – now a highly relative concept – are discarded. This process in turn reinforces the attractiveness of youth, impelled by fear, as outlined above. The effect-complex is further reinforced by feedback from old and young and the functional cycle of aesthetic innovation.

In two ways this functional cycle produces as a side-effect the image of youthfulness as a general paradigm – an object of voyeurism, and of sexual desire in general. First, from the position of capital, which can only valorize itself through regular aesthetic innovations, young buyers are particularly ideal because they respond quickly to what is new, and are malleable and suggestible in both an active and passive sense. Second, at the same time, it is they who constantly develop new forms and styles and offer a base of subculture from which capital can draw inspiration for fashion renewal. Most of all, some opposition groups among the young are highly productive for capital in an informal way. They consider their lifestyle to be set apart from the establishment; in so far as they make questions of appearance in lifestyle a point of criticism, they continually develop new appearances which are for a time their own – intended to identify them as a group – but which are constantly expropriated. Each new trend of aesthetic self-expression among the young automatically opens up a new market which, from the standpoint of the capitalist market, function as a testing ground. The commodity images which are a hit in this market are adopted *gratis* by the manufacturers, in the sense that the commodities on this experimental, and often informal market, act as a kind of pilot commodity for capital. In so far as these trial markets and commodities are developed among youth's sub-cultures, the original sign of youthfulness is left intact when large-scale capital takes over and transfers them to the general market.

By promoting an aesthetic innovation taken from this source, with the aim of out-dating a certain category of still-usable commodities, and thus reopening the market through the power of sensual temptation, youthfulness itself is simultaneously promoted. Intensifying youth as a guiding stimulus, the functional cycle is once again reduced. When adolescents are used as the paradigm, the related propaganda for aesthetic innovation scores a hit indirectly by way of their behaviour. Whatever they do will be copied and manufactured.[72] Thus a particularly ideal customer becomes a general customer-ideal. This is why so many concretizations of capitalist valorization lead to the same side-effect: the orientation towards youthfulness.[73]

Youth becomes a stereotype not only for commercial success but also for sexual attraction, and thus for what appears to be happiness and success. Another vicious functional circle is established. At first there was the fear of being abandoned by capital because of one's age. This fear was 'cured' capitalistically by the offer of commodities promising to impart youthfulness. But soon this newly set standard of youthful styling could not be adhered to without the adult appearing bizarre, and facing rejection. What began in the earning sphere of a growing army of employees finally came to determine sexual attraction, and not only of those who were useful to or rejected by capital according to the youthfulness of their appearance. Now being young equalled being sexually attractive. As a result, with the threat of sexual ageing and thus isolation, there spread a universal compulsion for people to 'cosmeticize' both themselves and the interiors of their homes. The commodities with which large firms 'rejuvenate' their range, in order to reinforce and exploit this tendency respond in their aesthetic promise of use-value to this blend of social and sexual fear and desirability. They offer themselves to the buyer as a kind of sex-object, a manifestation of the desire for youth, as a means of preparing one's appearance to attract attention and expectations of others similarly conditioned to youth-fetishism, or at least not to scare them off with signs of ageing. Each commodity, however, fills one gap while opening up another; each commodity and sale entails a further one. This dynamic has a totalitarian tendency, which is striving for totalities founded on whole generations of commodities.

Terms like 'total fashion' or 'total design', devised by the agents of capital, are inadequate to reveal the totalitarian teleology of this dynamic. For they still only touch on the aesthetic relations between certain types of commodities, such as ladies' fashions (clothes, wigs, cosmetics, accessories), or interior design (furniture, carpets, curtains, lamps, vases, pictures, etc.). As in the social world where different generations coexist, so the 'styles' from the commodity world cover a sector of the market in which one commodity-generation replaces another. Among the styles designed for the young and those buyers oriented to the youth-image, this change of generations is especially swift and thorough in replacing each new thing. Unlike the human world, each generation of commodities comprises an entire 'product family'. In living rooms, matching curtains and wallpaper betray signs of one designer. Once decided upon, the commissioned design creates ever-changing interiors out of one mould; the only determining factor is that they must look new, as if from one mould, and tempting. Such a commission leads to the formal perfection of designing where the design itself is a matter of indifference. This contains a compulsion towards subjective arbitrariness, which itself arises objectively from the constraints of capital valorization.

In the field of design, the expression of ideas is not the central issue. This lies in creating ideas in the ever-changing disguises of protean capital. These 'creative people', as the designers who serve capital's amorphous aims call themselves, are turned into mere shadows of creative people. What they make is always already reappropriated into the pointlessness of a mere façade, which is itself immediately replaced by the next. On the other hand, it is the very meaninglessness of capitalist design which gives it unlimited freedom and the greatest impact. The negative aspect of capitalist design appears as a tremendously exaggerated positiveness; its poverty looks like abundance. The fact that this design does not arise from human needs for useful objects, but solely from the requirements of capital valorization and its instrument of aesthetic innovation, is expressed in its modern style of design, under which useful objects cannot maintain a rational and familiar continuity. If one takes its use-function as its rational kernel, then every use-function within capitalist design provides an opportunity to use design techniques. Wherever possible, new commodities grow up around these opportunities. Any functional aspect of a room or house is seized on by 'design', and its surface fancifully distorted as if in a Disney cartoon. One's home becomes a 'landscape'.

'A new lifestyle demands new interior ideas. Möbel-K . . . turns them into a reality,'[74] announces the all-colour catalogue of a furnishing company, itself a triumph of colour-printing. This functional cycle: lifestyle→interior decor→realization in commodity form, represents less than half the reality. What appears to be the cause – the lifestyle – is more likely to be the effect. When capital develops and realizes 'ideas' out of the public's current needs, then those needs won't know what's hit them, especially since only the sectors whose needs can be made 'satisfiable' by commodities are selected. Elements of emotional unbalance from which the furnishing company shaped its ideas for interior landscapes were obviously new sexual trends, aimed both at married couples and at sexuality outside the confines of marriage, which has emerged since the dissolving of puritanical bourgeois morality, articulated openly especially among the dependent middle class. The 'new lifestyle' – a parodied renaissance of a *vita nova* – is seized upon by furnishing capital as a sector of the market to which special commodities can be offered.

This interior landscape thus becomes a landscape of sexuality. The catalogues so often included in bourgeois newspapers even present inhabitants of this landscape. For example, one such is called 'Angelika – furniture for sophisticated lovers'.[75] Between mirror-tiled walls, on large round divans, on deep-pile shag carpets simulating animals skins,[76] or on an equally idyllic mossy glade, young naked bodies are displayed – not just man and woman but also woman with woman, only male homosexuality is omitted. The interior landscape, into which a whole family of commodities has been integrated, is no longer just decorated with sexual symbols, as the single commodity usually is but it is surrounded by a whole complex of commodities which become the environment of one's sexual life. Whoever possesses such a home expresses an objective desire, through the physical properties of the setting, for a corresponding lifestyle, whether they subjectively desire it or not. These induced patterns of behaviour mirror the whole process of being presented, seeing and being seen. This place is 'sexy' to the extent that an earlier version was 'cosy'. The induced atmosphere of lasciviousness, rich material and concealed lighting, are as inclined to undressing as the people in the catalogue. Sexual instincts are already anticipated in this interior landscape, indeed they are its chief characteristics.

Even if inspired by emancipatory desires uncovered by capital, and transformed into a commodity as interior decor, once this sexual landscape has been purchased, because it promises the buyer sexual satisfaction, it will create an instinctual structure no longer identical with the original 'idea'. The owner's instincts will be inexorably drawn to populate this empty sexual stage with life, namely their own. He or she will have to fill the scene with suitable company, i.e. sexual partners. And this will not be the only acquisition, for we must not forget the numerous accessories, such as a cocktail bar and alcohol, both necessary accoutrements for enlivening the sexual landscape. This landscape requires its bodies to be placed in easily visible positions. The lighting, harmonized with the rest of the fittings, must be able to illuminate every nook and cranny of the body. And the scene demands bodies that do not smell and who are always available for inspection. Consider how many purchases must be made, how much work done, before a body is properly prepared for viewing – a whole range of cosmetics is needed for a start. Once more the path of the youth cult comes full circle with this landscape, which demands bodies without fat, wrinkles or deficiencies. Not that the scene is really concerned with the young, its participants are more likely to be adults attempting to appear youthful and beautiful.[77]

In such an interior wherein bodies are reflected, not much other reflection goes on. Behaviour such as work – except on the image – or political discussion would be completely out of place in this context. In this home no one grows old and no one is ever sad. Any anxiety, not to mention melancholy, would seem sinful and forbidden. Apart from life amid the gleaming bodies there is one alternative close at hand – the ultimate elimination – death. Whoever wants to grow old and survive such a setting would have to shed it like a cocoon, transferring from one design to another, like a buyer abandoning one sector of the market for the next.

7   Commodity aesthetics – its comprehensive meaning;
    'Hush Puppies' and the spread of the fashionable dog;
    subject–object relation as conditioned by commodity
    aesthetics; natural history of capitalism

In 1943, as a wartime economy measure, the US Government required the meat industry to introduce new skinning methods for piglets, as the basis for the valorization of the hides in the leather and footwear trades. One leather and shoe company developed machines specifically for this purpose. This enterprise grew into one of the world's largest shoe empires – Wolverine World Wide Inc., Rockford (Michigan) – which sold more than 120 million pairs of shoes between 1959 and 1971 under the trade name of 'Hush Puppies' and the basset-hound symbol. Since 1963 there has been a licensed subsidiary in the Federal Republic which, up to 1971, had sold more than 6 million pairs in that country alone. The reason why the company does not run out of pigskin, 'which is after all only a "waste product", is due to the continuing popularity of barbecues which cost the lives of millions of American piglets.'[78] The brand symbol, the dog and the name, is known to more than half the people in the Federal Republic, and by as much as two-thirds of the under-thirties, and is thus known to more people than most 'well-known' politicians.

In answer to the question of how the company arrived at the trademark, they tell a story worth remembering as revealing evidence of the capitalist spirit. In 1958, somewhere in the American Deep South, the sales director is said to have come across a group of people eating popcorn, and throwing some to their barking dogs with the words, 'Hush puppies!'. Watching this scene, a good idea came to him. It might profit his firm to offer something to pacify another kind of noisy 'dog'. This, of course, was the public – the world of buyers. During consumer research potential buyers were given seven names from which to choose. 'Hush Puppies' scored lowest. Yet the name was selected because it pleased the retailers, on whose sales business the company now depended. The point is that the 'user' came last in the sales department's calculations, and success has proved them right: the user's judgement could easily be remoulded, and bought off by the dog-symbol.

The trademark's success is reflected in the approval of *Frankfurter Allgemeine Zeitung*'s business section. 'This endearing little chap,' they wrote about the basset-hound trademark, 'who seems a bit of a clumsy fellow but lovable from the moment you set eyes on him, with his long brown ears and white nose, now has friends in over 46 countries.'[79] Without this disguise, the greed for profit which pacifies people like barking dogs would never have so many friends from all over the world. The animal suggests a quality of shambling loyalty intended to buy off and silence the buyer's reasonable mistrust. The immediate results of this promotion were hugh profits and a rapid growth in Wolverine capital. But there was another achievement, by way of a by-product. The breed of dog used to sell commodities was at the same time promoted and became very popular among dog-lovers. 'The basset became a real fashion dog in some countries.'[80]

The incidental promotion of a type of dog resembles the breeding and encouragement of human behaviour. The critical assessment of commodity aesthetics, therefore, is not restricted to analysing the aesthetic styling of commodities. These subject–object relation-ships of people under capitalism can be analysed in so far as they are determined by objects in the form of commodities, whose aesthetic appearance is functionally designed from the standpoint of valorization.[81] As we saw in the previous section, the totality of commodities from a furnishing company goes far beyond the 'total design' which gives them aesthetic unity. Not only do they involve whole groups of commodities from other market sectors but they breed modes of behaviour, structure perception, sensations, and power of judgement, shaping our language, clothing, and under-standing of ourselves, our attitudes, and above all our relationship to our bodies. This is why reports of commercial success from mass-consumption producers are also bulletins from the frontline of human moulding. The impetus to this lies in the profit motive and, to adapt Brecht, one could say, 'You think that typhoons are shocking? Wait till capital is out to get its profit!' (Brecht actually says, 'Wait till a man is out to have his fun!').[82]

But this sentence is all too short; the full horror only emerges when capital drives a wedge between people and their enjoyment by exploiting for motives of valorization their desire for pleasure. Wherever there is a need or a fear to be encouraged between the poles of money, sexuality and security, the opportunity will be seized. It sets in motion the following mechanism. Out of a com-plex of needs a segment is cut which is possibly 'satisfiable' with commodities. Then commodities are developed whose appearance and symbolism fit the selected need like a key in a lock. The targeted buyer is then confronted with articles in which unsatisfied areas of the consumer's being seem to find perfect expression and satisfaction. The instinctual response to these things is employed to turn human beings into buyers. If they cannot help but reach automatically for the goods, it is because the promise and thus the illusion of a life superior to their own, with which the agents of capital have made these things, has been stolen from them, the people who have become their buyers. Now they give up their life and strength in labour, in exchange for an illusory use of their own life. Suitable segments of what is felt to be lacking are given extra-positive treatment in their aesthetic presentation as commodities. The exploited structure of needs has been remoulded in the process. Paralleling the permanent aesthetic innovation in the world of commodities is the permanent change of the system of needs. The direction of this change cannot be unequivocally discerned, but it undoubtedly reinforces basically irrational inclinations which are completely incompatible with an articulated class-consciousness.

There is quite a difference between asking what use a thing is and whether it is saleable. The first question corresponds to the essence of the use-value standpoint, and only in socialist society will it become the decisive question. The second question is the essence of the exchange-value standpoint: the trend which brings to the fore the phenomena of commodity aesthetics and takes them to extremes, and which is based on private commodity production and can only be transcended with it. So long as saleability regulates production along profit lines, both objectively and subjectively, only saleable objects will be developed. From the standpoint of all ideal values, at which point the bourgeoisie made its historical appearance (thus immanently criticizing this standpoint), no further progress can be expected from a late-capitalist society other than towards the further corruption of humankind.

If one tries to sketch developmental trends in commodity aesthetics under late capitalism, there are at least two which can be forecast with some certainty: where its quantity and implicit meaning are concerned, the phenomena discussed here will increase; as for its quality, the effect will be that the use-value structure of commodities will shift further towards an imbalance of its relation to fantastic and imaginary needs. More and more commodities will change in a direction towards the extreme of the empty 'symbolic' article. This term is meant to convey that the degree of reality, and the essence of the commodity-body as a use-value, is shifting away from being simply 'an external object, a thing which through its [physical] qualities satisfies human needs of whatever kind',[83] towards an increasing emphasis on representation and symbolism in the commodity. The balance will shift from an unmediated, materially purposeful use-value to thoughts, feelings, and associations, which one links to the commodity or assumes that others must associate with it. Just as the packaging and advertisement of the commodities are attended by an entourage of associations, equally these need-related associations will be moulded into the commodity's use-value. Thus it becomes ever more important to see what points beyond the commodity itself, for example, positive and negative relationships to other commodities, its 'meaning' and 'sense' being based on determinants outside it. If the specific attraction of a commodity is, for example, its newness, then its quality already contains the negation of the old and in its quality it is transcended differently. It is thus not a simple affirmation but, depending on the meaning of newness, a negation. If its form results from the calculations of aesthetic innovation, one of its inherent qualitative features will be the 'out-dating' of the 'old'.

To say that commodity aesthetics moulds human sensuality is nothing other than, by the use of temptation, to throw light on to the method by which people are brought to conform to the capitalist system. They experience their existence in society as if it were an apolitical natural state. They are not coerced into their happiness; each can attain salvation in their own way. They turn away spontaneously from material necessities towards the satisfaction of their immediate needs, or any other temptations. The social relevance lies in the concrete polarization of need and satisfaction, but for the individual this aspect disappears since, under this system of concealed despotism in private ownership the individual's needs are enslaved and he or she believe themselves to be the active cause of their own behaviour. By avoiding material hardship, individuals appear to be perpetuating their own survival rather than that of the society. They pursue their own satisfactions and give in to temptations, while it appears that to do so is to pander to one's own elevated desires and not to share in social interaction with nature. The elements which attract the individual in a commodity's aesthetics are deeply rooted in their sensuality and emerge as the spontaneous individual urge. In so far as these processes that mould sensuality happen, as it were, behind one's back, they seem to be natural, characterizing history as natural history, a continuing and overdue prehistory of human society.

While we are discussing the growth and natural-historical character of these developmental processes in human sensuality and the world of commodities, let us return for a moment to the implicit reference to biological processes. The instinctual forces in these conditions are such that their overall functioning results in blind mechanical developments. The comparison of the multi-coloured temptations in the commodity world with flower-blossoms is easily made because both appearances have a *quid pro quo* in common.[84] For the plants it is the combination of the bloom's shape and colour with the scent and the nectar that attracts the insect. By obtaining nectar it performs incidentally the act of pollination necessary to the plant. For the plant, the process is essentially fertilization; for the insect, it means food. The bloom's attractiveness, arising from its 'beautiful illusion', through form, colour and scent, mediates in the plant's reproductive process. But the system in general would not work without containing nectar as a reward.

So far the comparison is, on one hand, much too orderly while, on the other, it neglects to show the dynamism of natural growth. The harmony disappears as soon as we look at a form which is based on and takes for granted the general validity of the reward system for insect fertilization. These are the carnivorous plants. They imitate the sensual attraction of nectar-bearing flowers, using this deceit functionally as a seductive illusion which the insects fall for – to their death.

Whoever calls this 'natural', as is the custom in such literature, does not omit to describe the creativity and power of the jungle, the fascinating, rampant, and mesmeric 'beauty', where the law of eat or be eaten is expressed and develops its weapons. One aspect is the universal struggle for survival, one against another, for food, territory and sheer existence. In as much as the fight is universal, everyone is involved in the struggle for new survival techniques. In as much as the threat of individual death or even the extinction of the species looms behind it, all the forces of 'nature' urge on this development. In as much as the life-forms act with or against one another, an ecological system develops to establish the levels of survival which the individual must face whether they like it or not. The accumulation of these forces of 'nature', mechanical and blind in their effect, is beyond the power of the helpless individual to influence. The aesthetic attraction within this organic 'natural system' is but one among many strands of survival.

On the level of commodity aesthetics, the development of capitalism presents itself as natural history, in as much as the universal antagonism of capitalists, seeking the appropriation of surplus value, creates a world of multi-coloured surfaces and manifold forms which as functions as bait for the buyers and their money. Now this insatiable hunger, and the reproductive drive of this

'Hydra-headed monster', whose every mouth snatches as much as possible from the next, is taking up a position behind the sensual world, and its corresponding system of subjective sensuality.

One capitalist individual outbids the other with the most glittering illusion, acting as a pimp between buyers, their needs and desires and material wealth, in order of course to attract buyers as merely transitory owners of temporarily abstract and scattered wealth. So long as there is money, no garment will fit the individual whim more snugly than capital itself. Nobody can outdo capital in fantasies, which it extracts from the masses, and turns into commercially suitable fantasies of the moment. When the chain reaction works, i.e. the commodity is a hit and brings in the returns, then subjective sensuality will have changed along with the commodities; and the success of this development is effected through the power of socialized nature, which is an expression of the fetish-character of the commodity and of capital. If the commodity in Marx's formulation is a 'thing which transcends sensuousness',[85] wherein 'sensuousness' indicates use-value and 'transcendence' the intangible social character of the economic determinant of form, then it is this transcendence [*Übersinnliche*] in the commodity whose power moulds and remoulds its own and human sensuality.

On the consumer goods market, all material devices are arranged for the capitalist individual and its agents in such a way that they can only gain access to abstract wealth by the deployment of commodity aesthetics. This decentralization into different spheres continues to unlease immense productivity. Thus the sensual human species develops passively in the grip of these pressures, as if it were a natural growth. Although each step offers the expectation of satisfaction, evolution rolls on without people becoming aware of what is being done to them.

Chapter Four

1 The influence of commodity aesthetics on the
  working class

The working class exists in relation to capital not only as those who
are exploited in the production process, as the creator of all values,
even of those which are the sources of all forms of profit and social
surplus: to the sectors of social capital which provide the necessities
of life, they are also a mass market of buyers. In the face of the
world of workers as buyers and consumers, the capitalist searches,
according to Marx in the *Grundrisse*, 'for means to spur them on to
consumption, to give his wares new charms, to inspire them with
new needs by constant chatter,' and this passage is important in
discussing the question of creating new needs. Marx continues: 'It
is precisely this side of the relation of capital and labour which is an
essential civilizing moment, and on which the historic justification,
but also the contemporary power of capital rests.'[1] In any analysis
it is of the greatest importance not to lose sight of this aspect of
capital's present-day power base, especially in theories of absolute
manipulation, illusory satisfaction, etc. Nevertheless, it can no
longer be said that by multiplying further or producing fashionable
varieties commodity production lends capitalism an historical justification. This could only be discussed in the context of further
developing the productivity of labour. This is an area where capitalism still makes progress which, as far as society as a whole is concerned, amounts to increased possibilities to save labour. Of course
only a fraction of what could reasonably be achieved is realized
under capitalism. The development of the USA, the leading capitalist power, shows dramatically how any advance in productivity
within a capitalist framework helps to increase the destructive
potential of this mode of production, and leads through crises and
wars to the destruction of capital as well as society's productive
forces in general. Technical possibilities are sabotaged, the army of

the unemployed and destitute grows continually (these are partly absorbed into the armed forces), which leads to destruction in a double sense, to the mass slaughter of foreign soldiers and their own decimation on the battlefield. On the surface, the Federal Republic of Germany seems to be different. Instead of murder, the class struggle – if we overlook the first indications of possible change – is waged by means of slander and defamation. Instead of waging its own imperialist wars, the state supplies materials and finance for others' imperialist wars. In 1971 the army of unemployed had almost vanished, and down and outs are seldom seen since they are carefully hidden away in ghettos. Even now mass consumption seems to prevail.

The Federal Republic achieves a special status by the direct competition of systems with the German Democratic Republic.[2] The apparent victories of capitalism in the Federal Republic can be explained by the ruling class's fear of socialism. This fear constitutes a contributory factor to numerous decisions from company to State level. The path to open violence in capitalism in the Federal Republic is blocked by the mere presence, just across the border, of the GDR. But the path of corrupting gratification remains open. One stage along this path is purely material satisfaction, another is continuous exposure to the seemingly apolitical propaganda for commodities, articulated in the language of temptation, needs, instinctual fears, of envy and of a compelling self-comparison with one's rivals.

The conscious, political moves on the part of the working class to heighten the conflict between wage-labour and capital, which is determined for the workers by their relationship to the sphere of production, is opposed by a secondary relationship in which workers confront capital as part of the world of buyers and consumers. This is determined by the sphere of circulation so long as no crisis overtakes it. In the first place the principles in this sphere are derived from the exchange principle, and the relationships determined by freedom, equality and justice. Freedom here means freedom to enter into contracts, and freedom of choice. Equality means that theoretically everyone enjoys the same freedoms, although of course this is restricted materially to how much money each has available; equality is also irrespective of the persons involved, merely respective of money. Justice, finally, means equality of what is given and what is taken away.

The problem with the justice of the transactions within the sphere of circulation is of course what Marx analysed as 'secondary exploitation'. Significantly, he remarks on this in the context of 'the renting of houses, etc. for individual consumption.' And Marx continues, 'it is plain enough that the working class is swindled in this form too, and to an enormous extent; but it is equally exploited by the petty trader who supplies the workers with means of subsistence. This is a secondary exploitation, which proceeds alongside the original exploitation that takes place directly within the production process itself.'[3] This offers the sole economically based starting-point for a theory of 'exploitation via consumption'; and although the New Left favoured such theories for a while, they omitted this particular aspect while, for instance, campaigns attacking extortionate rent rises originated from this argument.

Despite secondary exploitation, which seems to affect equally all members of society in so far as they are buyers, the conditions under which the working class as buyers in the circulation sphere come into contact with capital have taken on the illusion of classlessness. The evidence that the agents of capital are aware of the immense propaganda impact of this illusion of classlessness, which covers all fields of commodities, can be seen in the fact that they have established a kind of self-censorship in their own advertising and other published material, which ensures that no individual capitalist betrays the class nature of the social relationship. This was demonstrated, for example, by the allergic reaction of the *Frankfurter Allgemeine* to an advertisement 'which had already elicited a bad response deep into the political sphere'. The advertisement, by an American air-conditioning firm and thus addressed mainly to capitalist customers, showed an anatomical sketch of the human body with the caption: 'The worker is a modification of the human being. His particular constitution (muscle power) enables him to participate directly in the production process.' The *Frankfurter Allgemeine* devoted a whole column to this advertisement in its financial section.[4] First came the invective: it was 'stupid and thoughtless', created by people 'out of touch with the world'. Then the origin and character of this world: 'Decades of social development in this country, which puts people with their psychical and intellectual aspirations at the very centre of the economy, are simply ignored as if nothing in the appraisal of the worker had changed in 70 years.'

Where preserving the illusion of classlessness, or at least of harmony between the classes is concerned, there is in this exceptional case talk of a 'worker' [*Arbeiter*], rather than 'work-*taker*' [*Arbeitnehmer*]. Only in the propaganda, for which 'ideology' would be a eupheimism, are *people* at the centre of the capitalist economy. However thanks to certain important stages in German history during the last 70 years, in particular the era of National 'Socialism', as well as the capitalist monopoly of the mass media, this propaganda has been extraordinarily effective.

Now for criticism of the advertisement itself, where we must respect the columnist's artistic use of language, since he has to express something without actually mentioning it, and so must speak the language of camouflage. 'Such a degradation of the working person to a mere production tool is not only thoughtless but downright stupid.' Note the subtlety. Not *wrong* but stupid! For here we are dealing with a dimension of the class struggle in which the property-owning class and their agents are fighting vigorously for the consciousness of the working class. The systematic illusion carefully created by the agents of capital of 'people with their psychical and intellectual aspirations at the very centre of the economy' has been damaged by the Americans' advertisement, so that the worker subjected to wage-slavery, threatens to become visible from under the idyllic surface. The criticism concludes with a hidden threat of sanctions: 'The doctrine that the firm's image in the public eye is vital to the success of an enterprise was first brought here from America.' And there follows a very broad hint. 'In the face of repeated criticism of the irresponsible behaviour of US firms in the European sector – remember the IBM affair in Hanover – they might be expected to be a bit more careful with their publicity.'[5]

In the sphere of circulation, only the money in customers' pockets is important to capital irrespective of the customers' class-position, and it is precisely in response to this that in commodity aesthetics there dominates the illusion through which a particular class culture tends to integrate the workers – the capitalist distortion of a classless culture. The ethereal vault above us is becoming less and less heavenly – except perhaps in the sense of blue holiday skies – less and less determined by eternal ideas and rights, art or the Fatherland. Nowadays it is one huge supermarket in which, outside the sphere of work, the social world of this capitalism changes. An illusory totality reigns in the supermarket, which not only tries to determine the meaning and sensuality of each commodity, but also those of people and their social relationships.

Not only has the individual holding out against this all-embracing artifice no meaning, but this realm of beautiful illusion disputes the meaning of class and class consciousness, the individual's only standpoint for holding out. The illusion which communicates opposition to the contradictions between capital and wage-labour is not just deceitfulness but it has a place among the constantly renewed attractions of commodities, facts, things, and objective relationships. Despite being merely an illusory solution of that basic contradiction, it is an objective one. To survive this illusion, the class consciousness of the worker must be able to see through it and recognize it as propaganda. For capitalist propaganda in the field of commodities operates simultaneously as propaganda for commodity production. It triumphs when the wage-dependent masses accept it, and thus their own fate as a class, as natural; when their perceptions have grown so accustomed to propaganda, which objectively scorns them, that they notice with sadness its absence on the streets of socialist countries; when they reject the political slogans on socialist factories, or even socialist propaganda altogether as an imposition.

The power of commodity propaganda does not result from manipulation in the sense of shallow advertising images and general titillation alone, but its real kernel lies in the commodities' use-values and their general availability. The proletariat are unable to maintain class-consciousness against the satisfaction of their own needs. Just as commodities in the sphere of circulation represent the hard core of propaganda, without which propaganda would be treated with derision, so the 'commodity-craving', in its concrete form of wage demands in the sphere of production, provides the hard core upon which class consciousness is established. The total negation of the commodity world and the aesthetic miasma with which it envelopes people cannot, because of the legitimacy of the above relationships, be regarded as a viable starting-point.

2   Comparison with socialism to clarify specifics of
    commodity aesthetics under monopoly capitalism; the
    influence of commodity aesthetics on socialism

In the food markets, for example in the German Democratic
Republic, one can look in vain for the use of commodity aesthetics
in competing colours and packaging for the same class of use-
values. This occurs because under socialism the form of commodity
production is subordinated to an overall plan in which the product's
form is reduced to an essentially insignificant element, with the
result that we are already dealing with an economy designed to
answer needs – a use-value economy, characterized by standardized
goods available from any shop. The commodities are standardized
in that those of competing firms do not appear to differ within a
certain type and quality of products. Now, where use-value is
rescued from its subjugation by exchange-value resulting in a standard commodity, the real differences in quality are emphasized.
Socialist competition relates to productivity (or fulfilling the Plan!)
and grades of quality. Naturally, new problems arise for which new
or better socialist solutions must still be found. More and more
depends on possibilities of determining needs, which precede production and enable it to be orientated to those needs.[6]
   Further problems arise from the broadcasting of advertisements
for the capitalist commodity world, as, for example, in the form of
advertisements on TV in the Federal Republic. Just as commodity
aesthetics affects the working class under capitalism, in the same
way it operates under socialism as propaganda. Especially since
they lack the experience of actually being deceived, many, in the
slipstream of propaganda, feel betrayed by socialism. The devious
ways of a dulled memory are illustrated by the widespread reaction
to the appearance of a commodity, in this case a tin of food. The
jars or tins in which the food is kept seem, at first glance, to have
been produced with economy in mind – one label provides a
description of the contents. There were comparable appearances
under monopoly capitalism during the war, when the wartime state
economy guaranteed capital a huge demand which out-stripped
supply, making commodities scarce and so commodity aesthetics in
many sectors became superfluous. The packaging, the second skin,

correspondingly withered away. This regression, due to the disappearance of any economic function, determined for the masses the image of tinned foods during the war. It is thus within the context of general anti-communist propaganda that the GDR is rejected by many people today because they say that it reminds them of the war. This is because the packaging and styling of socialist commodity production no longer have the same function, which determines them under capitalism.

The aesthetic composition which in the Federal Republic is called 'design' (in the language of its motherland, the USA), originates under socialism from a political decision, as does anything to do with the economy. It is not just a by-product of a particular function or system change nor a natural outgrowth, but subject to consultation which sometimes involves the Party. Or production collectives decide what they think is right. In the GDR questions of composition lead to decisions which have a specifically socialist political form.

Although the superficial appearance of many commodities in a socialist society is markedly different from that of similar commodities in capitalism, it must be stressed yet again that the interest lies primarily in the functions which determine these phenomena and not in the surface of the appearances. The point in criticizing commodity aesthetics lies not in criticizing the appearances and techniques it uses as such, but the important point is that certain economic functions take over and assimilate these techniques, which in principle were developed well before capitalism and which have also been developed in non-commodity-producing societies. The techniques are turned into vehicles of the function, and this process of assimilation then becomes the impetus behind the transformation of the assimilated phenomena.

If one overlooks the functional determination, one could easily end up adopting an attitude which resembles the inconsequential weakness of pacifism, where all violence is rejected on principle, regardless of whether it be used for oppression or liberation. There is a difference between a gun used in an imperialist war and one used in a war of liberation. One cannot tell from the gun itself. Its detached and reproduced sensual impression does not reveal the essential difference but serves to disguise it. 'The situation thus becomes so complicated,' Brecht says in his analysis of the

Dreigroschenprozeß, 'that a simple "reflection of reality" tells us less than ever about reality itself. A photograph of the Krupp works or the AEG imparts almost nothing about these institutions. The true reality has been shifted to the functional.'[7]

One cannot tell the difference between a struggle for liberation and an imperialist campaign of plunder and genocide by looking at the rifles. To speak out against imperialism is not to inveigh against guns, but to help the liberation movement obtain arms and allow them to denounce imperialism. And it is the same situation in criticizing commodity aesthetics. It is not directed against the frippery on certain articles but, on the contrary, it reveals how an unrestrained economic function of capitalism is sweeping across the sensual world with the fury of a natural disaster, destroying everything that does not acquiesce, and assimilating and expanding certain features it comes across into a position of domination in order to strengthen and secure the domination of capital.

3   The derivation of the most general social fate of the
     instincts under the relations of private production of
     commodities; the warping of sensuality and aesthetic
     fascination

We must investigate more thoroughly the position of human sensuality in the exchange society, so as to isolate the general determinants, which are also fundamental in analysing the further development of aesthetic relationships between subject and object under capitalism. These determining factors can be derived from the relations of production. Our task, therefore, is to derive the basic influences on subjective and objective sensuality in bourgeois society from the laws governing the private production of commodities by division of labour.

The question is how to approach the derivation. The answer, given at the beginning of *Capital*, proves to be anything but incidental even to our question. Yet one is often advised when reading *Capital* to skip the first part as it is 'too philosophical'. This advice is understandable in so far as the beginning presents great difficulties which have to be overcome; yet, remarkably, the difficulties are not to be found in the text nor in its subject matter, but in the rather curious relationship of the reader to the matter under analysis. The analysis encourages the reader to insights which require a change of consciousness, and this meets opposition from the reader. This opposition can be understood in one way as the subjective result of the historical process during which the logic of exchange was established and developed; or it can be seen as the unmediated reflection in the person's consciousness of this process's objective results.

An example of the whole complex of equally objective and subjective difficulties might be the radical differentiation and separation of use-value and exchange-value, the first problem posed by *Capital*. The contradiction between these two moments of the commodity recurs time and again at all levels in the theory of capital and in the capitalist system itself; these radically separate concepts are in their contradiction constitutive building blocks of ever-more concrete theories as *Capital* progresses. Commodities as exchange-values contain 'not . . . an atom of use-value', an assertion which is an affront to the general bourgeois consciousness, which reacts against it with resistance.

This is not the place to show how the concepts which Marx analysed in the first chapter are of truly fundamental meaning for all levels of the theory of capital, and how they are built upon. Here we are interested in the analysis of exchange, in so far as it affords a way into the analysis of this resistance.

Each act of exchange equates disparate qualities (use-values) according to a certain quantitative proportion (exchange-value). This equation radically *abstracts* from the multivalence of the sensual quality; by reducing all sensual qualities to mere quantities, it negates the sensual independence both objectively and subjectively. The question of 'How much?' as regards exchange-value must not only accompany the idea of any sensual object to enable it to become a commodity, but it must be able to dominate it.

From the lessons of the first chapter of *Capital* it is well known that the beginner has great difficulty in *not* accepting this equation of sensual inequalities in exchange as simply self-evident. Marx, with all his didactic skill, makes a point of emphasizing the scandal of comparing incomparable measures. He is forced to employ alienation techniques – in the Brechtian sense – in order to do so. For to the general consciousness, exchange and its accompanying logic are as self-evident as nature itself, and they form the second-nature of exchange society.

Marx demonstrates that the equation of sensually disparate objects themselves *cannot* have a sensual basis, but that it presents the culmination of basic social interaction amongst members of a society, sensually mediated via commodity inter-relationships in the act of exchange. Marx has to work against the 'natural' consciousness of the members of the exchange society, for their social relationships as such do not figure in the exchange. Any trace of them is wiped out by money. People are not conscious of the operation's rational kernel, they act without knowing why, and the relationship is realized 'behind their back'.

The basic structure of the exchange-society is at the same time both rational and irrational, although at different levels and in different forms of appearance. Inside narrowly defined limits of irrational factuality, the behaviour of commodity producers at first sight seems rational. They are producing for the market. It is within this framework that they tend to calculate their overall behaviour. Ultimately, however, the market cannot be reckoned with and is, therefore, irrational at a higher level: that is where judgements are passed on their deliberately rational activities; 'a relation which, as an English economist says, hovers over the earth like the fate of the ancients, and with invisible hand allots fortune and misfortune to men, sets up empires and wrecks empires, causes nations to rise and to disappear.'[8]

If this continual oscillation, which threatens innumerable groups with destruction or actual annihilation while others are unduly rewarded, eventually creates a balance, the result in terms of society would be a general reproduction in the form of numerous uncoordinated and private transactions. This result is produced *as if* the production has followed a plan. For the commodity producers whose commodity reproduction is successfully mediated by the market, a higher degree of rationality results. But the manner in which this result is achieved, 'behind the back' of the unaware individual, is irrational. This irrationality is all-embracing, dominating and incorporating as a moment the limited rationality of market production; and the resultant rationality of successful commodity reproduction remains incidental and external to the market. The typical mediation between private division-of-labour production and overall commodity reproduction in an exchange-society is not its real purpose; its own inner dynamism reacts against the resultant rationality with periodic crises. The system is structured in such a way that it owes its regularity to incessant crises, its order is based on destructive chaos, and its law operate as 'the law of gravity asserts itself when a person's house collapses on top of him'.[9]

Under socialism, however, social rationality is made concrete to all in the priority production has over the consumption which, after all, it serves. The priority of production as well as its determination by human needs are guaranteed by the plan and the political organization responsible for it. The effort involved and the restrictions imposed on the individual by the prioritization of production (with all its difficulties and occasional wastage) are, from the point of view of its instigators, both intelligible and rationally based, even if insights into its necessity, and its consequences for socially adequate behaviour – for the socialist personality, in short – cannot be produced automatically, but only as the result of prolonged political and economic endeavour.

In the exchange-society it is through commodities that producers haphazardly enter into relationships, or rather, they delegate their relationships to the commodities. Their social relationships take the form of a relation to, and distribution of, things: their products slip from their hands and start a life of their own, with unauthorized overall social consequences which put the producers in a position of inferiority, so that in this social movement the fruit of their endeavours – the commodities – gain power over them.

Now we must attempt to develop from these most general social determinants those of fundamental importance to an analysis of the aesthetic relationship between subject and object. In a society in which crucial relationships are mediated by commodities, as by things which are highly differentiated in their sensual aspects and at the same time equivalent in value, specific contradictory modifications in the sensuality of members of society take place. An ambivalent conditioning from birth teaches the individual to submit their behaviour, and thus also their perception of objects of desire, to the dominance of exchange-value, by which objects are so manifestly directed in their existences. The underlying motive for this submission to exchange-value is the need-driven intention to share control over the vital necessities of one's own life.

The dominance of exchange-value enforces on members of society a specific form of self-control, very different from the rational discipline of a socialist society. Endeavour and results are not immediately connected, since results in an exchange-society entail irrational consequences, which at any time can assume the form of an arbitary fate or, less often, the winning lottery ticket. The necessity to which individuals must bow in order to get their share is only formally intelligible, not inherently so, because it has been dramatically hammered home on every side: it is only obvious *that* one must submit, while the inherent reason remains impenetrable. Precisely because the system compels submission to an irrational necessity, it compels not just a quantitative disciplining of sensuality, comparable to the concept of 'delayed gratification', but also its qualitative warping.

Brecht illustrates in his *Seven Deadly Sins of the Petty Bourgeoisie* what is meant by the 'warping of sensuality'.[10] It is the story of the seven stages by which a woman becomes rich in a capitalist society. In the end she is wealthy but broken in spirit, 'so tired':

> and grew envious of others:
> Of those who pass the time at their ease and in comfort
> Those too proud to be bought –
> Of those whose wrath is kindled by injustice
> Those who act upon their impulses happily
> Lovers true to their loved ones
> And those who take what they need without shame.

In the answer given by bourgeois reason, the reasonable is just as entangled with the unreasonable (although the latter is being rejected), as the state of affairs in the economic structure of bourgeois society. Bourgeois reason says:

> Sister, be strong! You must learn to say No to
> The joys of this world, for this world is a snare;
> Only the fools in this world will let go, who
> Don't care a damn
> Don't care a damn –
> Don't-give-a-damn will be made to care.
> Don't let the flesh and its longings get you.
> Remember the price that a lover must pay

And say to yourself when temptations beset you –
What is the use?
What is the use?
Beauty will perish and youth pass away.

The fifth stage in the suffering of sensual spontaneity is called 'Lust', since, viewed from the standpoint of exchange-value, love appears as lust. The story of the fifth stage is a double plot with dual solution. This is the plot:

Then we met a wealthy man in Boston
And he paid her a lot because he loved her
But I had to keep a watch on Annie
Who was too loving, and she loved another;
And she paid him a lot
Because she loved him.

A loves and pays *B*. *B* loves and pays *C*. This is the double solution: Anna gives up her beloved in order to keep the lover and his money; her lover holds on to her more than his finances will allow and thus ruined, he puts a bullet through his brain.

Even in the ghastly irrationality of the prevailing bourgeois reason, elements of rationality cannot be avoided. Simple commodity production, and above all, capitalism, are the historically necessary precondition not only for the intellectual possibility of such a critique, but especially for the only concrete alternative to capitalism. When we take a critical look at the 'warping of sensuality', we do so not from the standpoint of a retrospective glance at some Golden Age of sensual spontaneity. The emphasis on 'becoming' could be misunderstood as the glorification of what might have been. The standpoint from which we can criticize the characteristics of reason and sensuality in capitalist society is a form of reason and its relation to sensuality which arise from an insight into what is needed in regulating production communally.

The warping of sensuality in bourgeois society is followed closely by the sensual fascination induced by commodities. For every commodity producer is in competition and, as such, no more than a legalized bandit of exchange-value. 'Each person speculates on creating a new need in the other, with the aim of forcing him to make a new sacrifice, placing him in a new dependence and seducing him into a new kind of enjoyment and hence into economic ruin. [11] The contradiction of interests between different people as bearers of differing, economically pre-programmed roles, who personify the contradictions between the use-value standpoint and the exchange-value or valorization standpoint, exerts a deep and contradictory influence on the formation of subjective sensuality. [12] The poles of this contradiction can now be investigated in greater depth.

It is crucial for the exchange-value standpoint's relation to its objects that, despite the sensual differentiation of an object, attention is constantly focused on the quantitative uniformity of the exchange-value. From this point every object is potentially a substitute for another, or for the object of currency which stands for all others – money. Every sensual characteristic and all material independence has always already been annihilated.

To the same degree that the object's sensuality is negated, so also is the owner's sensual relationship to it, and every relationship must be simultaneously negated and confirmed, in order that one may take possession; this is what is meant in an exchange society by being in control of one's senses. Training oneself in self-control, as indifference is the only sensual conditioning appropriate to the exchange-principle, is the prerequisite for the realization of social relationships which causes a reaction from exchange-society within the life of the individual.

Directly related to this sensual conditioning is the conditioning of the human faculty which questions the meaning and purpose of the individual's daily practices as well as those of the community. This faculty – reason – is diffused into a socializing process of the instincts, in the course of which reason dissolves into an unconscious rationality engaged in calculating and working out every stage of the individual mediations. This involves a highly abstracted logic (nevertheless limited to a narrow area and disappearing in late capitalism), which deflects towards infinity any concrete question as to its sense or purpose. Thus reason justifies the dominant irrationality of the relations of production, controls the rationality suited to irrational constraints, and creates mystification on the orders of the highest authority. (Even amid such mystification, reason still makes its claim and acts as a critic, a function which the system of increasing irrationality cannot afford).

If the relationship between needs and objects is broken, the latter are rendered interchangeable and non-sensual, being only disguises for exchange-values; while on the other side the sensualization of the non-sensual occurs, since exchange-value has taken on its own individual shape, essentially independent and qualitatively different – a form of use-value in itself. This is in effect the objectification of the disembodied, the unitary object which governs needs in their non-unitary, disrupted relationship to objects, like a dazzling golden fetish. Yet even before this shape of the hoard that Marx called 'its aesthetic form, the possession of commodities made out of gold and silver',[13] is recognized as a disguise of use-value and is reduced to a mere passing phase, finally turning into a predominantly idealized factor in the valorization process of capital, the exchange-value standpoint becomes fixed in this independent form of exchange-value. Thus the miser becomes a creator of wealth. From the standpoint of valorization, this may seem a childish way to accumulate treasures, but it still constitutes an important means of creating a subjectively moral bourgeois dictatorship over the subject's senses, and is thus inseparable from a dictatorship over the individual's critical questioning of meaning and purpose.

> In order that gold may be held as money, and made to form a hoard, it must be prevented from circulating, or from dissolving into the means of purchasing enjoyment. The hoarder therefore sacrifices the lusts of his flesh to the fetish of gold. He takes the gospel of abstinence very seriously. On the other hand, he cannot withdraw any more from circulation, in the shape of money, than he has thrown into it, in the shape of commodities. The more he produces, the more he can sell. Work, thrift and greed are therefore his three cardinal virtues.[14]

Enmity towards the senses is the hoarder's absolute safeguard of the subjective basis. While the moral sages and economists of old saw society as threatened by the domination of money, 'modern society . . . greets gold as its Holy Grail, as the glittering incarnation of its innermost principle of life'[15], this principle of life is no less than the return of the exchange-principle into the structuring of human subjectivity, of course in its various historic manifestations.

By accepting exchange-value as an end in itself, at first subjective and arbitrary in the person of the miser, and then in capitalism as the objective impetus and material independence of the valorization process, this pursuit of individual aims destroys their own fundamental meaning. It is only an illusion that the individual is pursuing his or her own aim. Yet this illusion has become the strongest feature of capitalist society, and floating above it is the miasma of the apparently gratified sensual needs.

If commodities seen from the standpoint of exchange-value are only disguises of the exchange-value, the logic of this standpoint creates ever more enticing disguises which expose and arouse the desires of people as potential buyers, thus both opposing and reinforcing the individual's training to be indifferent to them. Within this same context of abstracted sensuality a function originates, (for the commodity, a distilled sense impression, put together in isolation according to all the rules of its art), which focuses on the mere appearance of use-value, that promises so much to our needs. Now this aesthetic abstraction (because it is beyond the confines of objective reality, a wildly flourishing, evergreen, yet fruitless sensuality) returns disembodied to affect the individual's instinctual and perceptual mechanisms. All this is a consequence of the fetishistic character of the commodity, of the mode of production where commodities function, as Marx put it, as 'sensuous things which are at the same time suprasensible or social'.[16] If those things, whose commodity form and independent function bring such consequences, were merely sensual objects, products which satisfied needs, or use-values in a planned economy, such a backlash would have neither place nor function.

According to each person's class position, the poles of the contradiction – fundamental to an exchange society and an historical force for change in capitalism – are accentuated differently. Their destructive dialectic discharges itself in periodical attacks on productivity, in order that, during prosperity, they can develop as a process of creeping corruption. The subject of economic enterprises, whose aim is to seize a share of society's surplus production, displays a different sign of self-control from the subject in wage-labour. When the means of valorization, having become an end in themselves, take on an individual as a functionary of capitalism, his or her original driving aim will remain different from the individual's existence as an agent, even if it only exists, unarticulated and dormant, within other recesses of that person's being. Although accepting valorization as an end in itself implies aspiring to its means (and suppressed aim) and accepting opportunities of success not open to the ordinary wage-earner, at the same time the capitalist functionary subordinates the aim to those related means.

To the wage-labourers it can hardly be the question of exchange-value as such, as it is for the capitalist, which lays emphasis on the fruits of their labour. The commodities available for individual consumption assume a disproportionate importance when they can provide meaning to a life spent largely in wage-slavery. The attractions of commodity aesthetics, as a contradiction and pacifying, rewarding contrast to the pressures of production, have a quite different effect on wage labourers than on capitalists. The more irrational the enforced sacrifice of sensual demands appears from the position of class, the more important the reward in the shape of commodities becomes for stability. In this situation where one natural force opposes another, stability is only made possible when an already dominated sensuality supports the domination of other's senses. In a situation of highly developed productive forces, the temptations offered by commodities know no bounds. Since unmediated social motivation cannot exist in the capitalist system (unless it be an illusion created by the ruling class for their victims, adopting many guises and for different purposes but operating under the general label of 'serving the community') these anodyne trinkets help to perpetuate the continually fascinating motive. Thus forced into a state of indifference, people fall victim to the fascination of commodity aesthetics.

4 Collective praxis and the illusion industry under capitalism

In Venice a picture postcard is on sale which advertises both the city and an American company. It shows St Mark's Square, empty of people, but with its famous flock of pigeons. The pigeons are sitting in an organized shape: in huge letters they form the name Coca-Cola. The letters are those of the 'copyright protected' trademark design. The lay-out for the advertising photo was achieved by the advertising manager hiring casual labourers to spread birdseed on the square in the shape of the trademark. The pigeons did not gather with the intention of forming the trademark but to satisfy their hunger. But equally the seed was not scattered to feed the pigeons but to employ them on its tracks as extras. The arrangement is totally alien and external to pigeons. While they are consuming their feed, capital is subsuming, and consuming, them. This picture, a triumph of capitalist advertising technique, symbolizes a fundamental aspect of capitalism.

Capital mobilizes a huge army of wage-dependent workers. Under its command the division of labour and cooperation reach higher and higher levels of society, the workers moving along lines laid down for them by wage-dependence. In a capitalist society, anything beyond their required wages, which represent their share of consumption, objectively will not, and cannot, be satisfied. The way they are organized in the sphere of production as a production-collective is not their own doing but a matter for capital itself. Their productive power is alien to them, and their production reproduces this alien power on an escalating scale, and with it their own dependence on this alien power. Their collective activity – their praxis on a social scale – has no collective meaning, but only the private and impoverished one of their individual reproduction as wage-labourers. The interest which governs their social praxis is profit interest and this has only a formal connection with private interest. The same term applied to the class of wage-labourers and to the capitalist class takes on a meaning as different as robber and victim.

The equity of exchange between wage-labour and capital is a mere illusion. For the mass of producers, cooperation in society for private interest has no social meaning but merely reproduces new generations of wage-labourers, for whom the meaning of wage labour is just that – wages: it atomizes them, and yet it is they who form the basic productive force on a *social* level. Their social character has been taken from them and appropriated by capital. Thus social content and private capitalistic form contradict one another.

The same applies to collective activities which take place outside the immediate sphere of production, in a very special 'sphere of consumption', namely during wartime. Even here we find collective cooperation *par excellence.* War, Walter Benjamin stressed,[17] is the only possibility within the range of capitalism of fully employing the productive forces that have developed within society without destroying society. The full potential of cooperation between members of society from all the productive forces can only be realized under capitalism in the form of war.

When the workers become discontented with their unceasing labour for the alien power of capital, they are pushed towards a political class-consiousness. Thus those whom capital has organized socially, create their own organization as a class. Socialism in this sense means the emancipation of already socialized labour from the domination of private-profit interests. Only if labour in society is organized in the general interest of society can collective praxis become collectively meaningful. The highest form of objective collective meaning under capitalism is the class interest of the workers, in so far as it manifests itself in the concrete form of political praxis and organization. The feebler and more stunted the class consciousness of the majority of wage-labourers becomes, the less they will sense a need for a collective meaning in the collective processes they take part in.

Such processes can only be meaningful for wage-labourers if they are suited to each individual's purposes, at the same time following personal aims and having a collective significance. If class con-sciousness is raised, it may be that workers will express the sense-lessness, or even the paradoxical nature, of the collective actions in which they participate, in acts of sabotage. This was the case when, during the Nazi period, social democrats and communists in certain factories sabotaged torpedo guidance systems so that they would miss their targets. Within the collective action, a certain practical conclusion drawn from class consciousness and the contradiction of interests is that one must take action. It is a kind of reasoned decision to take the destruction of a central part of the production process to absurd lengths. Under capitalism collective actions, i.e. which move beyond the private sphere and objectively fulfil their preconditions, that is actions which correspond to the social hier-archy and to the unmediated social interests of all people determined and organized by them, are alien exceptions to the system. The nearest thing to such action is the prevention of natural disaster: fires or floods which have not affected us personally are, for this very reason, quite popular, since they allow the normally isolated masses to form an ad-hoc community. Yet whatever is saved from flood or fire becomes once again private property, and property relations are re-established. The high degree of satisfaction the masses can derive from their communal action in averting catastrophes, is therefore largely fictional.

Not only does capitalism induce a constantly frustrated desire to know the meaning of the collective actions into which it coerces people, but while it is healing the wounds with one hand it is opening yet more with the other. It capitalizes on the satisfaction of these needs, albeit in a particular form which still requires investigation. Within the capitalist system, these needs can only gain an illusory satisfaction. For collective actions to be objectively meaningful to all concerned, capitalism must be transcended, and socialist relations of production established in its place, i.e. social activity must assume an immediately social form. Within capitalism, people's needs for an unalienated, non-property-oriented form of praxis, reappropriated to serve society as well as the individual, can only be satisfied in an illusory, artificial or even artistically dreamlike manner which displaces the very purpose of the activity. And as we all know there is a whole illusion industry hard at work constructing just such illusory satisfaction.

Since the vast majority of people can find no worthwhile goal within the capitalist system, the distraction industry appears to be a good investment for the system as a whole, as well as for competently run private capital. The need of those at the bottom to be distracted from this aimlessness meets the need of those at the top to distract attention from the dominance of capitalist class interests. From this springs an odd sector, whose administration moves from private-enterprise into state-capitalist hands. Adorno and Horkheimer have described characteristics of this sector, affording it a special investigation under the heading of 'The Culture Industry'. Of course, as in other works, both concept and theory provide scarcely more than a metaphorical interest in the critique of capitalist political economy, and they rebound in cultural pessimism. [18]

In the distraction industry the dominant interest is the one whose purpose has been displaced. The crime against the existing order which must be overthrown, and the seemingly meaningful pursuit of the criminal, exert a fascination precisely because they involve the public's stultified interest in a division of terminology suited to the system: the language of crime and prosecution. The most heinous bourgeois variant of the detective film – the psycho-thriller – which deals with the crime of destructive mania, personifies the meaninglessness of the system. It expresses itself on a larger scale as destructive irrationality, and projects the fear this creates into a pseudo-enemy which the rest of society, in an apparent show of general human solidarity, can pursue as a false substitute for meaningful collective praxis. Despite all their pretences, bourgeois war films offer good examples at all levels of these insinuations of pseudo-significant collective actions. The large-scale mobilization of productive forces and cooperation of high-ranking personages on a wide social scale are a constant feature. Isolated coexistence, persistent fear and competitiveness, and disguised class conflict, are sanitized by illusions into 'basic' friend-or-foe relationships; in dealing with the enemy destruction meets with destruction, while the 'goodies' cooperate, mixed with the occasional eroticization of solidarity and comradeship.

Many Westerns and war films are, at their emotional centre, about 'love between men', as a critic of the films of Howard Hawk put it. [19] An investigation of Western romance fiction in the Federal Republic revealed that the heroes of this literature are motivated neither by desire nor money but by 'justice', revenge for justice's sake being the most common motive in a plot. By and large, 'friendship between men is rated higher' than heterosexual relationships. [20] One precondition of this effect is that homosexual relationships remain latent, since only thus are they suitable substitutes for men's longings. These result from men's competitive existence which subjects them to a high degree of isolation. This is a general component of the male 'role', which allows men to break out of it in a kind of emotional solidarity, whose social implication must remain latent so that the displacement can obtain.

It is difficult for a member of capitalist society *not* to find these substitutes interesting, and *not* to let oneself be fascinated by them as a matter of course. [21] With shades and shadows the illusion industry populates the spaces left empty by capitalism, which only socialism can fill with reality. This is reflected in a peculiarity of the structure and content of television programmes in the GDR which seems odd by comparison with the West. The introduction of, for example, new agricultural machinery is given prominence as a new 'sensation' in collectivism, focusing on vital changes and improvements in working conditions; similarly attention is given to the introduction of new production methods in the industry, and the requirements for professional qualifications entailed by the development of new forms of collective work. And this is not merely featured in the news, for there has been a series of plays (*Zeichen der Ersten* is a good example), whose common feature is that crime, war, or some similar collective action, are no longer central, but rather the collective action which usually forms the context, and the conflicts, with their comic and tragic elements, all arise from processes which have now become political. These processes are in fact the collective organization of both production towards pure effectiveness, and of socialist cooperation, in which the interests of both individual and society in general come together, although not without tension.

When a capitalist concern applies a new production technique, as a weapon against the two or three other oligopolies in the field, it is not a political event but one born of competition, exploitation, and not least, of job-destruction. This, by means of a contrast, may explain why the concept of illusion industry is so particularly rooted in capitalism. For in the face of an all-embracing, social meaning in which the individual interest of all its members would be well looked after, capitalism has nothing to offer except mere illusion.[22]

5   Art owned by and in the service of capital (I): the commodity poetry of advertising vs the helpless anti-advertising of poets

Aesthetic form is put to the same use by capital as a respected work or an authentic expression. Wherever certain expectations of an objective kind and a certain attitude of receptivity are connected with artistic form, they can be exploited by advertising in the appearance of the commodity. Each moment of aesthetic production can be given a special function according to its exploitable potential. Art as a social institution, comprising endless collections of works with the attendant receptivity and behaviour patterns of the public (contemplation, veneration, collection, etc.), and as organizations (museums, exhibitions, art appreciation in schools, etc.), fares no differently. The more incongruous it seems to a naive bourgeois sensibility that the moments of this relationship should be used for the profane aims of capitalist self-interest, the more effectively such a sensibility can be deceived by these moments. A sobering as well as instructive example from religion, as an analogy with art, is the aforementioned case of the Diocesan Press which touts for advertising in *W & V* (an advertising and selling magazine), recommending itself as an advertising medium which works by transferring people's naive trust from pious texts and Biblical quotations to the adverts of commodity capital which would otherwise be viewed from the standpoint of the buyer with the usual mistrust.[23]

Painting, graphic design, and sculpture are similar areas of exploitation, as are music and poetry. In the case of blank verse as used in advertising we are immediately in the theoretically peripheral area which stylizes the verse written for capital's use, into a conscious aversion to the ideology of art. If Dieter Wellershoff had criticized traditional poems for demanding reverence, like the wearing of a Sunday suit, for their inherently ideological form 'and their traditional service of using education as a kind of exercise in commanding respect', he suggested that on the other hand the poem should be seen 'as the easiest and most flexible form of expression, the practice of free and individual speech that can be found nowhere else.'[24]

Wilhelm Genazino, however, cannot find much support among poets for this generalization which likens poetry-writing to activities such as swimming, dancing and contemplation.[25] 'Meanwhile this call for the free poem, a poem that can stand for anything and speak of everything, has been heard in other quarters. The poems which come from these quarters are printed by the million . . . they are what we like to call consumer poetry.' They 'don't describe a young girl's neck but the pleasures of smoking a cigarette (one particular brand, of course), not the atmosphere of an afternoon but the qualities of a washing machine.'[26]

However, their 'basic attitude' is not, as Genazino describes it in order to justify his term 'consumer poems', 'the attitude of direct consumer propaganda'. Rather, this impression is a mere illusion and a functionally determined moment of commodity aesthetics. Essentially we are dealing with the propaganda for certain brand-named products. Their lyricized 'qualities' are calculated to have a reliable effect on the motivation of potential buyers, but are only superficially related to the commodity-body's material constitution. It seems more appropriate, therefore, to speak of commodity lyricism. 'Their authors have taken the decline of the classic poem literally,' Genazino explains, and have thus 'given it a useful purpose'. This has probably been due less to the decline of the classic poem as art form than to the cash-powered demand of capital. Genazino expects the poem in commodity aesthetics 'to be less blatant than a slogan; to be quieter, and calmer than the deceitful posing of the slogan, and for this reason to have the appeal of a new honesty'.

This appeal should not be confused, as the advertiser intends, with the honesty the poem uses and the transference of expectations aroused by its subjectively sincere expression of our deepest feelings, which advertising is aiming at. The examples Genazino gives, however, show not only the appeal to honesty which is associated with the poem as such.

> The leaders advance
> In finance and in politics
> Just look
> at what they smoke
> then you know
> what they achieve
> They smoke
> G. R. André
> the New Brown
> Experience in Smoking
> Slim and cool
> Made
> for the leaders.[27]

On checking the material content, it is obvious that this is a lie: you cannot tell from their brand of cigar how the people in power achieve power. But the phrase 'the leaders advance in finance and politics', linked to the suggested choice of commodity brand as a symbol of their inclusion in the ranks of the powerful, does not dwell too long on an illusion of democracy, but articulates power, elitism, the complete permeation of politics and the state apparatus by capital. Of course this moment of enlightenment is over-compensated for by the recommendation that people buy their brand and join, symbolically, the power elite, thus reinstating the idea of 'equality', at least for the buyer. Enlightenment in this case means the moment of fooling the credulous, and the material 'honesty' of commodity lyricism turns out to be pure cynicism. This cynicism even goes so far as to betray certain mechanisms of profit-making, and proclaim the passive masochistic pleasure of surrendering oneself to them.

> A new beast is growing in our midst,
> Hunting across continents and leaping oceans,
> Racing as far and fast as it can.
> Claiming as many victims as possible,
> Entire nations succumb to it,
> And are left behind, torn, devastated,
> At least, the entire,
> Female population
> Of densely populated areas.
> The corruption rages on:
> Whoever is mauled and savaged,
> but once by this monster,
> Yearns for the next attack, the next bite.
> Such a delight in their destruction
> Makes the male population groan . . .
> FASHION,
> Particularly that aggressive sub-species
> THE FASHION SHOE.[28]

In fashion and its aesthetic innovations, which are as fast and as far-reaching as possible, we can see the strategy of the capitalist beast's hunger for profit, while human sensuality appears in the grips of the capitalist valorization process. So much for the 'enlightening' moments of this commodity poem, which appears to offer its reader no pretence but makes it appeal with a genuine honesty. The honesty is, of course, only an illusion, functionally determined, and necessary for masking the character of continuous

aesthetic innovation and inducing surrender. For aesthetic innovation does not appear in its capitalist functional determination
but as a rather enjoyable conquest of the public, especially women.
Once one has succumbed, one longs for the next attack. The
ambiguous statement that 'such a delight in their destruction makes
the male population groan', does not tell us whether they groan in
protest at, or in disdainful admiration of female passivity, or
whether it arises from the 'femininity' of the men themselves.

This aggressive propaganda was put out on behalf of the footwear industry in the Federal Republic. The aggressive attitude
becomes understandable when one recalls the crisis at Salamander
AG whose shares dropped to almost half their market value within
a few years. At the last shareholders' meeting, Fiebich, a speaker
well-known at numerous such occasions, accused the management
of having made insufficient use of aesthetic innovation, coupled
with decreasing the commodity's use-value. 'One should have
realized somewhat earlier that much more money can be earned
from less durable shoes.'[29] Apparently the depression does not only
make capital wax lyrical, but the difficulty of earning money in the
shoe trade leads to propagandist interference in human sensuality.

The examples above show that the form of the poem is being
used for particularly aggressive and cheeky advertising which takes
it away from the poets. 'Structure, verse and metre correspond to
the patterns of the modern poem, or at any rate to its avant-garde
examples (as Helmut Heißenbüttel remarks with mixed feelings).'[30]
The poet is not only suddenly faced with the return of the lyric
form as an advertising stereotype, but appropriated for nothing by
capital and functionally adapted to the requirements of advertising,
the form is becoming widely recognized as the powerful original,
against which the real prototype looks like a faded copy. Commodity poems, according to Genazino's completely uncritical
assessment, 'can be considered as the first poems in the West to
achieve a mass effect'.[31]

The lyric poets who have been thus expropriated and superseded
are trying to defend themselves with counter-propaganda, by
taking the abuse of form to its absurd limits and thus attempting to
attract attention back to poetry again. A volume entitled *The
Seventh Book of Advertising* is a collection of such attempts.[32]
Hilde Domin's contribution, for example is: 'Take a break/read

poetry/Poetry like love/makes time stop'. However, the inability to put up any resistance to advertising is rather pitiful. While advertising capital still has productive forces at its disposal, the poet may no longer say the same about language.

6   Art owned by and in the service of capital (II):
    representation of private enterprise

If commodity aesthetics takes art forms, artistic activity and the artists themselves into its service, its representation uses partly certain styles and partly certain works of art. The complex ways in which art is employed by private capital, joint capital and the state no longer fall directly within the realm of a critique of commodity aesthetics. However, since this complex is not only directly related to, but reflects something of the structure and operational laws of commodity aesthetics at a level which affects the whole of society, it should at least be offered as a concluding sketch. For in its representation, private capital, like capitalist society, adopts an appealing appearance which is supposed to have a legitimizing effect on all its important targets – on the political sphere, the money market and the workers. Here the aim is, as it were, to 'sell' capital as such and capitalism as a positive form of society.

In Friedrich Dürrenmatt's novel *Grieche sucht Griechin* [*Once a Greek . . .*], a junior book-keeper with the industrial giant, Petit-Paysan, achieves a rapid rise in fortunes through his association with an upper-class woman.[33] The name Petit-Paysan is a French rendering of one of the largest Swiss corporations, Bührle, which was named after a famous art-collector and patron who established an art collection in the city of Zurich. The company is heavily involved in the production of highly destructive weapons, but also produces some peaceful, useful goods: in Dürrenmatt's novel these goods are forceps. Recently the company has been involved in a scandal when it became known that they were smuggling arms on a huge scale. It was unavoidable that Bührle Jnr be brought to trial, and he was even sentenced to pay a small fine.[34]

As for the novel, the junior book-keeper *A.* is summoned to head office, a journey represented by his ascent within the hugh adminis-tration skyscraper.

A was entering unimaginable spaces, realms of glass and unknown materials, shining clean, with wonderful lifts which took him up to high and secret floors of the building. Perfumed secretaries floated past smiling, blonde, brunette, and a gorgeous redhead . . . tender corridors received him, with flashing lights now red now green above the doors, the only signs of any discreet activity. Moving silently on soft carpets, any noise, even the slightest cough, seemingly forbidden. French Impressionists glowed on the walls (Petit-Paysan's collection was renowned), a Degas *danseuse*, a girl bathing by Renoir, flowers spreading scent from tall vases. The higher they went, or floated, the emptier the halls and corridors became. They lost their functional look, super-modern and chill, without changing their proportions, and became more fantastic, warmer, more humane. Now Gobelins hung on the walls, golden Rococo and Louis XVI mirrors, some Poussins, some Watteaus, one Claude Lorrain; and when they reached the top floor . . . the book-keeper was received by a respectable grey-haired gentleman in an impeccably neat smoking jacket, doubtlessly a secretary, who led the Greek through charming corridors and bright halls filled with antique urns, Gothic madonnas, Eastern gods and Indian wall hangings. Nothing to remind one of the manufacture of atomic weapons and machine-guns . . . music vibrated from somewhere, Haydn or Mozart, no clatter of typing could be heard, no to-ing and fro-ing of anxious book-keepers, nothing that would remind him of the world he'd just escaped, and which now lay far beneath him like a bad dream. Then they stood in a bright room decorated with red silk, and a large painting of a female nude, probably the famous Titian that everyone talked about and whose price was whispered everywhere. Delicate furniture, a tiny desk, a small wall-clock which ticked silvery, and a little gaming-table with a few small armchairs were there, and flowers . . . They had scarcely entered when a small side door opened and Petit-Paysan came in, dressed like the secretary in a smoking jacket, and holding an India-paper edition of Hölderlin's poetry in his left hand, his index finger keeping the page.[35]

Dürrenmatt lays it on pretty thickly, as one can see: his 'prose-comedy', as he subtitled the novel, is rendered inoffensive by its use of exaggeration. The social indicators mentioned in passing are not overdone, but the author detaches them from the calculation of interests which underpin and maintain them. In any case the junior book-keeper *A* is intimidated. It no longer looks like prose-comedy when we find a description of the same effect in a training course report published in 1969. In it the recorded statement of a young industrial worker reveals the effect this use of art in his firm's representation sphere had on him:

> When I go into the directors' building, the stairwell decorated with stucco, oil paintings, and busts of some of the directors' ancestors is so impressive that by the time I reach the second floor I'm convinced that what the firm did in the past, does now, and will do in the future, is right and will remain that way.

In his formulation the spontaneously theological form is very noticeable: this is how we speak of God, and yet it is capital which arranges its own sacred setting and creates impressions which in Judeo-Christian theology are characteristically applied to God. The worker, deeply impressed, reacts accordingly. 'And when I want to put forward a complaint I feel like someone who's actually come to confess a sin.'[36]

In this representation the determining aim in the enterprise – profit – is hidden beneath the glamour of art. Capital, with art at its disposal, not only shows off as a connoisseur and admirer of Fine Art but also, in its esoteric interests, adopts the lofty illusion that it is the highest creations of the human spirit, and not profit, which is its determining aim. Thus everything good, noble, beautiful and great, seems to speak for capital. Art is used to dazzle, as a tool to create the illusion that the domination of capital is legitimate, and just as valid as the domination of the good, the true, and the beautiful, and so forth. In this way works of art can become a means, among others, of stupefying the public. They are deployed as one of many techniques of creating an illusory solution to the contradiction between capitalist private interest and the vital concerns of society as a whole.

Since this contradiction is as fundamental as it is all-embracing, it does not stop with capitalism's use of individual works of art. The function of illusory solution to this basic social contradiction, by expropriating 'high culture' or whatever is 'sacred', is to create a style: it permeates all the architecture of capital wherever it occupies a place in the public eye and emerges in the form of a building. The seat of finance capital appears as a Greek temple, the brewery as a knight's castle and the publishing house of the tabloid press as a Christian cathedral – places of worship for a pulp empire.

Even the employment of an entire architectural style, like the single work of art, is only one facet of the techniques this illusory solution to the contradiction uses. Large corporations try to set the scene for society using aesthetic props in the broadest sense, so that they might offer to society evidence of serving the public's vital interests. If the unscrupulous profit-making of the chemical giants poisons the environment then, threatened by a public outcry, the companies present themselves by means of fascinating colour photographs using the most sophisticated reproduction techniques, as guarantors of life, happiness, nature and progress.

In the 1971 shareholders' meeting of the Bank of America, who very profitably financed 35 per cent of the US troop transport to Vietnam, 'the Bank's President A. W. Clausen stressed "the increasing social responsibility of the Bank of America", especially when it was a case of "supporting racial minorities or protecting the environment". This year's report, Clausen proudly pointed out, was printed on recycled paper'. The reason for the Bank's efforts to 'give itself a youth-oriented image', and to make it appear as if it opposed war, can be seen, according to this report,[37] to rest on a series of attacks carried out on the Bank's branches by opponents of the Vietnam War.

If this annual report on its recycled paper seems like a satirical comment on America, then the company report in general seems to be liable to the same interpretation. The liberal *Frankfurter Rundschau* devoted a whole column to criticizing, in all serious-ness, firms which neglect the company report as an 'instrument of public relations'. The headline is composed as a slogan for aesthetic innovation: 'Grey Mice Out!'. The article begins:

> Business reports are annual visiting-cards from the company. Pretty colours and pictures make this fodder for shareholders more digest-ible . . . Of the three big successors to IG-Farben only Hoechst avails itself of the opportunity to dress the annual report in colourful attire. The enterprise provided its last report with over 50 coloured tables covering everything from the AGM to the dedicated workforce and the technical installations . . . from a sprinkling of sex to a veritable Venus in a bubble bath. The whole thing was appetisingly arranged, and served with the most sophisticated printing techniques.

The other IG-Farben successors on the other hand are criticized for publishing their reports without colourful pictures. The newspaper even expresses the class-politics behind the multi-coloured lay-out of the report, 'since nowadays it falls into the hands not only of a few auditors but also thousands of small investors whose expectations have to be met too.'[38] Not only the mass of workers but also the absolutely powerless small investors, who should really be called pseudo-shareholders, must be bought off with a colourful and dazzling illusion, if only in a different form and function.[39]

7   Stage-management and representation at a general social
    and state level, e.g. fascism as pseudo-socialism

Walter Benjamin in his famous essay 'The Work of Art in the Age of Mechanical Reproduction' has shown what importance the 'aestheticization of politics' had for fascism.[40] He pointed out the sophisticated construction of separating need from its expression and pompously developing the mere expression by aesthetic means against the needs and rights of the people. In his words:

> Fascism attempts to organize the newly created proletarian masses without affecting the property structure which the masses strive to eliminate. Fascism sees its salvation in giving these masses not their right, but instead a chance to express themselves.

And he continues in a footnote:

> In big parades and monster rallies, in sports events, and in war, all of which nowadays are captured by camera and sound recording, the masses are brought face to face with themselves. This process, whose significance need not be stressed; is intimately connected with the development of the techniques of reproduction and photography. Mass movements are usually discerned more clearly by a camera than by the naked eye.'[41]

After the footnote the text continues:

> The masses have a right to change property relations; Fascism seeks to give them an expression while preserving property. The logical

result of Fascism is the introduction of aesthetics into political life.'[42]

In his essay Benjamin seems especially fascinated by the influence of technology on social relationships and their connotations. On the other hand, however, he neglects the economic forms and functions, and in the work of his disciples this gap threatens to suppress completely the beginning of an economic foundation to the analyses. In the quoted passages above, the fascist aestheticization of politics is understood to be an illusory solution to the contradiction of property relations and the 'right' of the masses to change them. This false solution consists of engineering the aesthetic enjoyment and self-interaction of the masses in a way that helps to preserve existing property relations. Without doubt Benjamin has pinpointed the functional relation of aestheticization and the preservation of domination. But this insight needs to be developed, and extended in two directions.

1   It is not the technical apparatus which creates a medium of expression for the masses; it is effective only where a mere aesthetic copy can be used as a kind of amplification of the original. Rather it is the momentum of the masses, workers' struggles for higher wages, for limited working hours, against child labour, against arbitrary dismissals, for the right to work and – sooner or later as a necessary consequence – for socialism, that is, the struggle of many generations of workers which developed on the basis of their economically determined concentration in large industries, which created the many forms of expression that the stage-managers of fascism adopted. They made an aesthetic copy of the workers' movement, adding ingredients of petit-bourgeois and peasant nostalgia for the soil, blood-ties, guilds, carnivals, church, and ceremonies of consecration, and they organized it according to the latest insights, applying proven industrial and marketing techniques of social engineering, usually from the USA. In short, they created a political sphere from which all decision-making processes were removed, according to the Führer-principle, so that nothing was left but the mere phantom-like shell – its carefully

created exterior. And they converted this remaining political shell into a total work of art.

Two points must be mentioned here. Firstly, there is the position of the artist: many were finding work, a living, and fame, in the sudden demand from the state for window dressing, cult objects, stage-design, and representational art of a specific kind. To many who had known the horrors of extreme poverty this meant salvation. The historical result, of course, meant destruction for them too.

The second point concerns the after-effects still felt today of this large-scale aestheticization of depoliticized politics based on 'stealing from the commune' (Bloch). Its function in those days was to politically overwhelm the workers (i.e. the mass of employees, petit-bourgeoisie and peasants), by separating the expression of the working-class movement from the movement itself and its objectives, and by separately satisfying the declared needs of the workers by means of aesthetic fascination. These superficial 'borrowings' from the communists, therefore, were turned into weapons against communism, and rounded off the success of the Gestapo and the concentration camps. Today, after the destruction of fascism, this bygone technique of anti-communist aestheticization strangely continues to exist. When today organizations in the working-class movement or their sympathizers revert to using old forms of expression which fascism temporarily seized as its own during the Third Reich, the propaganda of the ruling class responds with a subtle move which many find difficult to see through. Since, naturally, there are many apparent parallels with the fascists – unsurprising since fascism aimed at surface resemblances – now that fascism is taboo, the left is equated with the fascists. In the equation, red = brown, the fascist version of anti-communism once again fulfils its function of bewildering the masses. Intellectuals who remain on the surface and who have an acute sense for creating effect, like Günter Grass, easily fall for this second-degree aestheticization, which they then propagate to the best of their abilities.

2   Benjamin's theory of fascism's aestheticization of politics must be considered more deeply from another angle. He overlooks

the high status of mere illusion in capitalism, an inevitable product of the economic basic relations, and originating fully in the economic structure of bourgeois society in its normal condition – if one dare calls its non-fascist constitution a normal condition. As has already been shown, the aestheticization of commodities is a necessary consequence of exchange. It is a fact that at all levels of the system in bourgeois society the people's vital interests are *neither* the highest objective *nor* the determining aim. To the extent that in the social relations corresponding to the different levels of social life it is necessary to make these relations appear to serve vital human needs directly and exclusively, the ruling class is forced to create a kind of expression and justifying scenario, to produce the illusion that social relations really do serve the vital needs of all. This illusion must convey complete classlessness, justice, humanity, welfare, etc. and/or make subjugation, service, discipline and sacrifice, appear to be natural and the highest fulfilment. Every expression which gains the trust of the masses or, in the jargon, 'has credit', will be brought into play and stripped of the concrete endeavours it once expressed. Hence it is necessarily the mere abstraction of an expression which is nothing other than aestheticization. The activities of aesthetics' producers meet this demand in its form, but *not* in its content, *nor* from the outset according to subjective motivation.

The aestheticization, not only of politics, lies therefore at the very heart of bourgeois society. Also intrinsic to it is the need on the one hand constantly to legitimize the ruling class, while creating the needs of their subjects on the other, both of which can find only the illusory satisfaction of amongst other things aesthetic images inside and through the capitalist system. But we must stress one fact: not everything that is a false illusion is a deception – only most of it. The additional factor, without which the social deception would not work is, of course, self-deception. The consciously-engineered technical deception, the political *ratio essendi*, that earns profits for many industrial giants today, could not work without the self-deception of the subscribers to the *Bild* newspaper. This self-deception, in turn, would not operate so smoothly without a whole chain of numerous middlemen whose business is deception and self-deception.[43] Without an opium of the people there can be no opium for the people. This can be applied to the world of pop music, as well as, *mutatis mutandis*, to the magic of Bayreuth and its representative holy festivals where, under the eyes of the cameras, the leading politicians rub shoulders with the tycoons, the bankers and the generals; where the personifications of power, domination and force appear publicly on the dizzy heights of culture.

Appendices

Response to an enquiry from the International Design Centre

'How should our environment be designed so that it deserves to be called human?'
Environment means a second nature. When someone talks exclusively about environment they are either leaving out a great deal or else pretending to be stupid to please those in power. Environment is the world over which we have no say and through which we should move like animals in the jungle – or in the zoo. When it deserves the name of a human environment in people's eyes, then they have come to terms with the struggle for existence. Then – to pursue the zoo image – the animals' cage has been pleasantly redecorated as a seemingly open wilderness.

Our world has been seized by capital, which rules and valorizes both it and us. The hunger for profit of big capital turns the world into a heap of commodities, private estates and rubbish dumps, with a meagre 'public sector', which continually bows to the interests of capital, squeezed in between. There is no effective planning in the interests of the population as a whole. So long as production and distribution are regulated by capitalism there can be no planning founded on an interest that deserves the term 'human'.

What people require, use and consume, where they live and move about to satisfy their needs, how they arrange their lives, decorate their homes, dress, make themselves attactive, and find others attractive and thus desirable – the totality of things, lands and people – are designed, controlled and exploited by capitalist interests. The only design, the sole plan, that matters for capital is the pursuit of profit. Things, land and people, are perpetual grist to the capitalist mill.

'What is the function of design?'
In a capitalist environment the function of design can be compared

to that of the Red Cross in times of war. It tends some wounds, but not the worst, inflicted by capitalism. Its function is cosmetic, and thus prolongs the life of capitalism by making it occasionally somewhat more attractive and by boosting morale, just as the Red Cross prolongs war. Thus design, by its particular artifice, supports the general disfigurement. Its responsibility lies constantly in questions of styling, in environmental styling. German fascism set up a number of state departments for such functions, such as the 'Department for the Beauty of Labour'. Thus design takes on political functions. When it styles commodities it promotes their saleability, and unmediatedly takes on a function in capital valorization. (Why is there no mention of this in the IDZ pamphlet?).

'What, in your view, can your school of thought contribute to the clarification of these problems?'
The contribution of philosophy could be in the form of efforts comparable to a lie-detector applied to society. In our society the left hand does not know what the right hand is doing. Philosophy could keep it better informed.

One cannot tell from the look of styling what its function is. Therefore, we must remind ourselves repeatedly which is the function and which the context.

The greatest problem of all is how to remould the world into our home. This can only happen through the socialization of the economy and collective planning of social labour.

From the postscript to the Swedish edition of 1975

Besides the interdisciplinary methodological and factual interests, it was the political element which made the Left-wing groupings in particular discuss this theory in different areas, more or less intensively, though often with great wariness.

Despite the varied and controversial reception the theory received, from our position today certain misconceptions can be seen, which were shared by its supporters as well as its opponents. This is partly due to lack of clarity in my text which helped these mistakes to occur. This is why I clarified the text at least at decisive points in the Swedish edition and eliminated outright errors. But perhaps it will be useful to mention the main misunderstandings in the hope of saving the Swedish reader extra work.

Many positive and negative appraisals of the *Critique of Commodity Aesthetics* were due to a major misunderstanding of what it set out to do. The book was received as if intended to be a kind of complete analysis of late capitalist society, and as if it wished to suggest a new strategy for the working class movement – or at least to give a new and practical perspective to the design trade.

These claims completely miss the potential use of this book. Commodity Aesthetics is just *one* functional complex, *one* aspect among others in our social reality. The analysis of commodity aesthetics provides *supplementary information*, makes a *contribution,* to understanding this social reality – and of course to aid the foundation or improvement of strategies and orientation within the progressive movement. As soon as this aspect is turned into an absolute, everything becomes lopsided. Then it might appear, albeit wrongly, that the *Critique* offered illusions of a 'non-class-specific consumer alliance', for which this book was in fact attacked; or, as in an assault from the other side, that aesthetics *as such* are damned by the book; and there were similar misunderstandings along these lines.[1]

On top of the misunderstandings appeared conscious distortions from interested parties: as, for example, in 1972 a TV film was made with the title 'The Beautiful Commodity Illusion', supposedly based on this book but unfortunately full of terrible mistakes. As the Central Board of Advertisers announced:

> This book is now willingly used by the advertising critics. Soon it will be carved up for a TV programme. For this reason it is important to stress what its author remarked in a (very small print) footnote on page 147: 'The lack of functional determination in commodity aesthetics within the entire capitalist process has led to a disproportionate emphasis on psychological aspects in these essays. This led me to the nowadays widespread overestimation of irrational human manipulability . . . The first of the two essays, especially, proceeds from muddled and inaccurately stressed economic assumptions.'[2]

What a masterpiece of manipulation! The Central Board misconstrues a collection of my earlier essays,[3] to give the impression that my self-criticism, relating to work published ten years earlier, is directed at the position I held in the *Critique* which in turn pro-vided the basis for the film. And then, perhaps realizing that self-criticism is not really a sign of weakness or dishonesty, and to get rid of this unwanted side-effect, they added the notorious 'small print', a practice which suggests the shady deals only too familiar from buying and rental contracts! Incidentally, it must have been a long search before they happened upon the very footnote they quoted. Had they not wanted to fish around in troubled waters, they could have had it much easier. As any reader can discover, I criticize my earlier essays in more depth (and in large print) both in the postscript to the above-mentioned collection and also on the opening pages of the foreword to the *Critique*. This self-criticism can confidently be made at the start, since the *Critique* represents a fundamental advance over earlier essays, and since it could hardly be accused of 'lacking a functional determination in commodity aesthetics within the entire capitalist process'. Its core, which has turned the *Critique* into an interdisciplinary paradigm, ultimately lies in its economic derivation of causal relationships in commodity aesthetics.

The newspaper which represents the upper-middle class in the Federal Republic – the *Frankfurter Allgemeine* – contributes its own 'refutation'. In the course of reviewing a book whose author had made an attempt at criticizing my theory,[4] it alleges (falsely) that I had claimed that commodity aesthetics was a remedy for economic crises; it proceeds to state (correctly) that there is at present an economic crisis in the capitalist industrialized countries; it then states (again absolutely correctly) that these 'cycles of crises cannot be countered by sales promotion in the sense of commodity aesthetics.' And it then concludes with razor-sharp logic that the foundations of my theory are wrong. The conclusion is straight out of the textbook – only the starting assumption is misrepresented, thus confusing the public. To round this off another stunning 'proof' is supplied (Watch closely, gentle reader!): 'The increasing unemployment among designers and advertising people . . . gives dramatic evidence that the foundations of Haug's theory are now out of date.' One might as well conclude, from the fact that at this moment hundreds of teachers cannot find work due to financial cutbacks in the Federal Republic, that the pupils' educational standards are already sufficiently high, or that classes are no longer overcrowded. But why do I say 'might as well'? It actually happens!

Now, in order to ensure the success of this attempt at returning 'the far-reaching critique of commodity aesthetics . . . to the limits of its birthplace, the sixties', that is, to bury it in the past, a great laurel wreath is carried to its funeral as a means of distraction, with a label saying that the 'kernel' of this theory lies in its 'merit' . . . 'of having composed with the sensibility of a poet, a modern history of human sensuality and the damage it sustains.' However, this wreath conceals a dangerous barb – the distraction from the real 'kernel' of the *Critique*, namely its economic derivation and functional analysis. If this opens up one of many approaches to a social analysis and a history of sensuality under capitalism, then it is not by any 'poetic sensibility' but by its method of economic derivation. For this reason the reader should pay particular attention to this method and check it carefully. It will then become clear that an economic crisis has no more outdated the foundations of commodity aesthetics than it has outdated the foundations of the economic forms of commodity, money and capital. Commodity aesthetics does not develop at the level of a national economic policy but rather at the level of the private commodity–cash nexus. It originates in simple exchange, develops in the course of private commodity production, and gains enormous influence in the monopoly-capital arena in the bizarre aesthetics of the monopoly commodity. Problems of turnover do not restrain but rather stimulate it, making commodity aesthetics a vital means of survival for every single commodity producer. This is why this same upper-middle-class newspaper can print report after report in their business section on aesthetic innovation brought about by crisis-induced competition, while at the same time rejecting the *Critique of Commodity Aesthetics* as 'out of date' in their review.

Small firms and entire industries are currently trying to achieve 'a new boom with the help of new fashion input', to extract 'impulse buying . . . from the new fashions'[5] and thus take the wind out of each other's sails. For example, Volkswagen made a hasty attempt to counter a fall-off in demand by 'stimulating impulse buying' with a complete aesthetic innovation of their models – and not without success. Of course the crisis in the entire economy is only slightly modified and in no way dispelled by such competitive efforts between enterprises, or by struggles between different industries for a larger share of the consumer market. This would be too easy a solution for capitalist society! But it is obvious that in any case commodity aesthetics is not a phenomenon of luxurious prodigality in a 'satiated, abundant society', but a normal and necessary function inherent in every purchase or sale. Of commodity aesthetics it can be said, as Marx did of the basic intentions of capital, that it springs from the 'inner being' of fundamental economic relations, and hence of capital, and is at the same time an 'external coercive force' regulated by competition between private capital. To recognize this is to grasp an essential aspect of social relations of private commodity production.

Being all the wiser from these misunderstandings, and alert to the more or less manipulative tricks of the capitalist camp, I would write the book differently today, more systematically and giving the economic derivation more emphasis. Gaps, too, would have to be filled out, especially in the transition from pre-capitalist to capitalist commodity production. It would be necessary to delve further and more systematically into the question of commodity aesthetics in the 'labour-power commodity' than was given in the example of the shop-assistant in chapter three. But these gaps can be filled by the readers themselves once they have mastered the economic section.

I wrote in the foreword that the concepts and functional analyses which this book has used for building blocks are readily available in *Capital*, Marx's 'Critique of Political Economy'. The ideal reader, therefore, is someone already familiar with the ideas in *Capital*. The reception of this book, however, taught me that an understanding of it in this respect is unfortunately not very stable. The best thing to come out of this is that many readers, after reading this book, have been motivated to read *Capital*. I will not deny that, in my opinion, any attempted analysis of our society will not get very far in all essential respects if one has not acquainted oneself with the fundamental, scientific achievements of the 'Critique of Political Economy'. The present book may serve as evidence that the *application* and further creative *development* of these theoretical instruments is not the same as the incessant quotation, to be found in certain writings, which seem to have substituted a glance at various – proxably very good – books for a hard look at reality. Application and further development of these basic insights can only be tested against material reality. But one misses the point completely if, like some liberal critics, one praises 'the scientifically accurate method' of my analysis and the 'substantial examples and up-to-date quotations', thus acknowledging my treatment of the material while trying to eliminate my debt to Marx.

Haug's analysis 'would be substantially more convincing if he had omitted most of the quotations he took from Marx' wrote one liberal paper.[6] But even if I had not once quoted Marx, my method and treatment of the material – acknowledged by the same paper – would still be chiefly indebted to Marx's *Capital*. Recently, in a special introduction to that work, I tried to expose the methodological achievements, and basic insights into the social context, which are still unique to Marx's major work, in such a way as both to facilitate its reception and increase its usefulness in contemporary analysis, thus making it independent of quotations.[7] In time, perhaps, this will also increase the number of 'ideal readers' even for this book.

If one were to indicate what this book chiefly owes to Marx's 'Critique of Political Economy', one would encounter a complex of relations which can be expressed from many different angles, but which all interrelate. Firstly, there is the genetic approach, then the process of 'logical' analysis of economic forms and functions; both aspects together make it possible first and foremost to define commodity aesthetics as an integral subject, and then to understand its development and differentiation together with its internal complex. The accusation from various quarters that the *Critique of Commodity Aesthetics* starts 'from the sphere of circulation rather than production' finds its answer in this method, which proceeds from economic forms and their dynamic, specific to certain relations of production. A third aspect that must be mentioned is the solution to the famous 'problem of mediation', in this case the mediation between the economic and the aesthetic; but even here Marx's analysis of value-form provides a scientific-historical paradigm.[8]

What can be achieved with the aid of the procedure merely outlined here, becomes immediately clear if one compares it with the assumptions and results of other methods. For this purpose, I will refer to what is probably the most widely read book to touch on the same subject as my own: Vance Packard's *The Hidden Persuaders* which can, in effect, represent a whole shelf of books on this theme.[9] Packard solves the problems of starting-point and procedure in an innocent, naively journalistic way. He reports on 'the application of mass psychology in advertising campaigns'. His approach is to collect statements from representatives of the advertising industry without differentiating any further between intention and reality, and then from these to piece together a picture of the indecent assault being perpetrated on the rational individual. Thus he achieves some good journalistic work by liberal standards, but his subject is determined more by a moral suspicion than by an objective analysis. For instance, he never considers the essential role of advertising and its campaigns. With these preconditions left unclarified, all the important questions are already decided in advance.

Most of all there is the initial assumption that there are good and bad advertisers, one who is undisputably normal and one who goes over the top and therefore must be rejected on moral grounds:

> Since our concern here is with the breed of persuaders known in the trade as the 'depth boys', much of the book is devoted to describing their subterranean operations. For that reason I should add the obvious: a great many advertising men, publicists, fund raisers, personnel experts, and political leaders, in fact numerically a majority, still do a straightforward job and accept us as rational citizens (whether we are or not). They fill an important and constructive role in our society. Advertising, for example, not only plays a vital role in promoting our economic growth but is a colourful, diverting aspect of American life; and many of the creations of ad men are tasteful, honest works of artistry.[10]

Right from the start this deflects any indignation towards advertising excesses, whose relation to normal capitalism is completely obscured: Packard does not as much as scratch the surface of the real causal relationships in this complex.

The *Critique of Commodity Aesthetics*, on the other hand, solves the problem of how to set about and define the subject matter, in such a way that its genesis and development can be traced from its origin. With an unprejudiced look at the simplest social conventions of exchange which, be it in the form of child's play and marginal phenomena, or from the daily experience of shopping, are familiar to us all, any member of society can recognize the basic law of commodity aesthetics. This law states that the motivation to exchange, that is to buy, is determined by the 'aesthetic promise of use-value', that is, by the use-value I subjectively promise myself on the basis of what the commodity objectively promises me.

This is the starting-point, the seed from which the ever-more-complex illusory world of commodity aesthetics developed and from which it is growing daily. To follow and analyse its development we need only to look hard at the standpoints containing the fundamental relations of interests, the manifestation of their opposition and the weapons that are therein deployed. There is no need for any special morality other than scientific honesty which entails the ruthless exposure of these relations as they really are. Of course, even the mere analysis of the situation immediately summons up the 'Furies of private property', that is, the manoeuvres of those who recoil from the light of publicity as soon as it illuminates their activities . . .

Notes

Author's Introduction

1 W. F. Haug 'Zur Ästhetik von Manipulation' in *Das Argument*, year 5 (25) (1963), reprinted in Haug, *Warenästhetik, Sexualität und Herrschaft. Gesammelte Aufsätze* (Frankfurt: Fisher-Taschenbücherei, 1972).
2 Ibid., p. 25 in *Das Argument*
3 Karl Marx, *Capital* (Harmondsworth: Penguin, 1976), vol. I, pp. 493–4, note 4.
4 Friedrich Engels, 'Preface to the English Edition', in Marx, *Capital*, vol. I, p. 111.
5 W. F. Haug 'Zur Kritik der Warenästhetik' a radio talk printed in *Kursbuch*, 20 (1970), 140–58; reprinted in *Warenästhetik, Sexualität und Herrschaft*; and 'Funktionen des Ästhetischen zur Scheinlösung von Grundwidersprüchen der kapitalistischen Gesellschaft', lecture given at the New Society of Fine Arts, West Berlin and printed in the catalogue to the exhibition 'Functions of Fine Art in our Society' as well as in *Das Argument*, year 13 (64) (1971), 190–213. Both essays are incorporated in the present work.
6 Norbert Elias, *The Civilizing Process* vol. 1 The History of Manners, trans. Edmund Jephcott (Oxford: Basil Blackwell, 1978); vol. 2. State Formation and Civilization, trans. Edmund Jephcott (Oxford: Basil Blackwell, 1982).
7 Max Horkheimer and Theodor W. Adorno, *Dialektik der Aufklärung* (Amsterdam: Querido Verlag N.V., 1947), p. 198. Translation by John Cumming: *Dialectic of Enlightenment* (London: Allen Lane, 1973).

Postscript to the Eighth German Edition

1   W. F. Haug, *Der Zeitungsroman* or *Der Kongreß der Aus-drucksberater* (Zurich, 1980), a satirical excursion into the political, ideological and commodity-aesthetic discourses of our society.
2   W. F. Haug, *Vorlesungen zur Einführung ins 'Kapital'*, 4th ed., (W. Berlin: 1985), first published in 1974. French translation: *Cours d'introduction au 'Capital'* (Geneva: 1983).
3   See the collection of my articles: *Ideology, Commodity Aesthetics and Mass Culture* (forthcoming from International General Press.)
4   W. F. Haug, '"Werbung" und "Konsum". Systematische Einführung in die Warenästhetik', in *Warenästhetik und kapitalistische Massenkultur* (West Berlin: 1980), vol. 1. The second volume, *Produktion, Warenkonsum und Lebensweise*, is shortly to be completed. A preparatory work to this second theme has been published: 'Automated Work and Labour Culture – A critique of the immiseration discourse' in *Ideology, Commodity Aesthetics and Mass Culture*.

Chapter One

1   Marx, *Capital*, vol. I, p. 209.
2   In the same way later, the capitalist will be handled while looking after his commodity-turnover and future profits, since advertising offers its services with the same 'most glittering illusion' even on tick: 'Advertise today, rake in the profits tomorrow and pay the day after.' Leasehold advertising is practised in the Federal Republic of Germany by the firm Leasing Werbung Werbefinanzierung für Handel und Industrie GmbH. 'Leasing Werbung,' explains its founding managing director, H. Hietmann, 'is the attractive way to put advertising on a hire-purchase basis. From our calculations we have discovered that quite a significant number of businesses and institutions are not able to advertise just when they really need to.' The interest rates should stand at 9.6 per cent per annum

as customers are mainly middle-class businesses. When they need advertising but cannot pay, they must promise this delightful company part of the attractive profits they expect, just as in the fairy-tale the miller's daughter promised her first child to Rumplestiltskin for spinning her straw into gold. If, however, the profit does not materialize or is less than expected, the noose tightens around the throat of the middle-class business until it breaks its neck.

3 These formulations partly quoted verbatim, partly paraphrased, come from Marx's section, 'Need, Production and Division of Labour' in the 'Economic and Philosophical Manuscripts' in *Early Writings* (Harmondsworth: Penguin, 1974), p. 359.

4 Advertising notices too began with groups of commodities which were 'put up for sale outside the usual channels of commerce or appeared unexpectedly on the market', that is with the particular and the new (Werner Sombart, *Der moderne Kapitalismus*, Munich and Leipzig: Duncker and Humblot, 1924) vol. II/1, p. 410. Sombart itemizes six commodity groups in which 'the advertisement acted as intermediary between buyers and sellers' long before the development of industrial capitalism: (i) books (since the fifteenth century); (ii) supposed remedies; (iii) new foodstuffs and confectionery (tea, chocolate, etc.); (iv) new discoveries (the telescope, wigs, hair-oil, etc.); (v) newly discovered imported commodities (almonds, sweet chestnuts, foreign wine – in England this meant French and Portuguese); (vi) bargains due to price reduction (caused by lack of storage space or imminent departure of the seller). Sombart concludes this catalogue 'with one word: no competitive advertising! The idea of competition is still alien to the business world'.

5 Marx, *Capital*, vol. I, p. 202.

6 Marx, 'Economic and Philosophical Manuscripts', p. 367.

7 See Marx, 'Economic and Philosophical Manuscripts', p. 358.

8 Ibid., p. 368.

9 Josef Kulischer, *Allgemeine Wirtschaftsgeschichte des Mittelalters und der Neuzeit* (Munich: R. Oldenbourg, 1965), vol. II, p. 27. Kulischer names as a source Franklin, "Le café, le thé et le chocolat", in *La vie privée d'autrefois* (Paris: Plon,

Nourrit et Cie, 1893), p. 109 f.

10   See Kulischer, *Allgemeine Wirtschaftsgeschichte* and Franklin, "Le café, le thé", pp. 1 f. and 76 f.

11   Bernard Mandeville, *The Fable of the Bees, or Private Vices – Public Benefits* (London: Wishart, 1934), p. 222.

12   Friedrich Engels, 'Preußischer Schnaps im deutschen Reichstag', in *Marx-Engels Werke* (Berlin: Dietz, 1963), vol. 19, p. 40. Engels uses this theme to expose the entrenched reactionary position of the landed nobility in the face of a social democratic proposal, based on the illusion of a social state, to save Prussian feudal absolutism from belligerent opposition. 'The only industry which still has excessively devastating effects – of course not on their own people but on foreigners – is the Anglo-Indian opium industry which poisoned China.' (p. 42)

13   Marx, *Capital* (Harmondsworth: Penguin, 1978), vol. II, p. 222.

14   Taking risks in business in turn creates more business. The services which the advertising firm provides should on the other hand insure against the situation wherein the value embodied in a commodity breaks its neck by becoming unsold stock. That the business of advertising is not always without risks, is proven by a Munich firm founded in 1971, Icarus Parachute Advertising, Film and Photos Ltd. It proposes as if by a magic ritual to take on the risk, acting in the place of the commissioning firm and removing the risk entailed, if this firm wants to sell advertising and public relations by means of parachute jumps. 'The founding partners are four German parachutists, who were encouraged to establish the business by the huge number of enquiries they received from industry.' (*Blick durch die Wirtschaft*, 25 August 1971).

15   Marx, *Capital*, vol. II, p. 208.

16   Walter Benjamin, *Charles Baudelaire, A lyric poet in the era of high capitalism* (London: Verso/NLB, 1973), p. 55.

17   *Printer's Ink*, 1905 quoted in David M. Potter, *People of Plenty* (Chicago: University of Chicago Press, 1954), p. 170 f. See P. Baran and P. Sweezy, *Monopoly Capital* (Harmondsworth: Penguin, 1966) p. 123.

18   Once the named character of a brand-article is established, then each commodity with this particular use-value, which

does not carry the brand-name and which supplies other distri-
bution-channels for the same company, will be known in the
future as an 'anonymous commodity' (cf. *Frankfurter Allgemeine Zeitung (FAZ)*, 23 September 1971, p. 14).

19 'Since United Fruit made the banana a brand-named article in
the Federal Republic of Germany in 1967, the company was
able to sell around 900,000 tonnes of bananas here.' (*FAZ* of
21 July 1971). In 1970 the Federal Republic imported altogether
512,000 tonnes. In the first quarter of 1971, banana imports
from United Fruit were 67,000 tonnes (against 44,500 tonnes
in the same period the year before). United Fruit's portion of
the market in the Federal Republic appears to be approaching
50 per cent.

20 The fact that the creation of a 'brand-name' has primarily
nothing to do with the product which must function as a
brand-named article, is strikingly demonstrated in the training
given to advertisers. At the former Academy for Graphic Art,
Printing and Advertising, their usual final projects took the
form of creating and advertising brand-names for articles
which did not exist. The projects were marked according to
criteria of a desired 'hit' in the selected target-group, even
when these criteria remained partially buried in formal
aesthetic values.

21 *Frankfurter Rundschau*, 23 June 1971. The article is based on
an enquiry carried out by the Institute for Trade Research
under the directions of the Federal Republic's Monopoly
Commission.

22 *Der Spiegel*, 5 (1971), p. 54 f, which also supplied the other
information on wine regulations.

23 *Der Spiegel*, 8 July 1964, p. 76.

24 Ibid.

25 *FAZ*, 20 July 1971, which also supplied the information on
the Deinhard case. From the standpoint of a brand-name monopoly – and this is the standpoint taken up by the journal of
the brand-name federation, *Brand-name* – it is a pre-requisite
'for the effective use of signs' that the whole system of signs
can enjoy the same protection for its brand-names and accompanying characteristics as for any private property. Recently
the standpoint of brand monopoly has been put forward by

Professor Kraft, whose partisan claims for his client's privi-
leges, like all blatantly partisan opinions, are rather enlightening. Taking a stand against the ruling on the 'Sirena' case from
the European Court of Justice, Kraft turned his objections
'finally . . . to the treatment which seems possibly to
discriminate between brand-names and patents which this case
had suggested. The commercial achievement that lies behind
every sign in current use is deemed to be of a different calibre
from, although in no way inherently inferior to, the achievement of someone who has legally patented the trademark.'
(*Blick durch die Wirtschaft*, 6 September 1971).

26 According to a German Press Agency report of 29 September
1970.

27 *Frankfurter Rundschau*, 10 December 1970. In 1970 a commercial turnover in excess of DM3.3–3.4 thousand million was
reported, of which only a part can be attributed to washing
powders. However, the calculation of advertising expenditure
as a percentage of a sector's turnover can be very misleading,
in that it could be disproportionately minimized. Calculated in
this manner, the advertising outlay of the company is related
to retail turnover, but this is apparently rectified when the
company carries out its own advertising for its brand-names
and thus addresses its potential buyers directly. However, if we
relate the advertising costs to the production costs, we receive
a radically different picture. Thus Chesebrough-Pond's Inc.,
in turnover the third largest cosmetics manufacturer in the
world, announced its figures for 1970 which showed 'that in
the consolidated balance with a net turnover of 261 (previously
231) million dollars, production costs (at 108 million dollars)
were for the first time lower than sales, advertising and administration costs (at 112 million dollars)' (*FAZ*, 14 August 1971).
Tucked away among these 'production costs' of 108 million
dollars – alongside costs for sales-promoting styling and
aesthetic innovation, etc. – are portions of the profit in a
hidden form, which means that these relations must be far
more dramatic than the proportions 108:112 would lead us to
believe. In the area of washing powders the portion of real
production costs must be even more effectively covered up.

28 *Tagesspiegel*, 6 November 1969, p. 20. The following figures

were also published here: 1968 annual turnover in food and confectionery: DM63 thousand million, followed by chemicals with DM44.8 thousand million and the engineering industry with DM44.5 thousand million. Two foreign companies achieved the largest turnover: Unilever with around DM2 thousand million and Nestlé with over DM1 thousand million, followed by the German company Oetker.

29 Willi Bongard, *Fetische des Konsums, Portraits Klassischer Markenartikel* (Hamburg: 1964), p. 25.
30 Ibid.
31 Ibid., p. 26.
32 Ibid., p. 25.
33 Ibid., p. 187.
34 Ibid., p. 28, note.
35 In 1970 more than DM3.7 thousand million was spent on advertising in the mass-media alone in the Federal Republic. The institute for advertising statistics, Schmidt and Pohlmann of Hamburg, discovered that this expenditure had risen by 8.8 per cent since the previous year. Retail shops in the Federal Republic invest about the same amount (i.e. about DM4.4 thousand million a year) in decorating the sales areas (*Frankfurter Rundschau*, 26 February 1970). All the expenditure on the image of the brand-named article and the company, and above all on periodic aesthetic innovations can scarcely be estimated. According to Baran and Sweezy's calculations, merely 'automobile model changes in the late 1950s were costing the country [USA] about 2.5 per cent of its gross national product!' (Baran and Sweezy, *Monopoly Capital*, p. 137). It is doubtless the case 'that the proven advertising costs are only the visible tip of an iceberg' (Carola Möller, *Gesellschaftliche Funktionen der Konsumwerbung*, Stuttgart: 1970, p. 24). According to calculations made by Fritz Klein-Blenkers, advertising costs in 1966 taken in the narrowest sense, 'without those costs which are hidden in other areas of expenditure', were estimated to total DM13.6 thousand million for the economy of the Federal Republic, i.e. 2.85 per cent of the GNP (Möller, *Gesellschaftliche Funktionen*). Möller sums up this objectively functional complex as 'commodity presentation', the entire costs of which can be seen as

the iceberg whose visible tip is the DM13.6 thousand million in 1966 and which, as a whole, we have called commodity aesthetics. Möller's concept claims to encompass 'the complete display of the commodity, beginning with its production form through advertising's creation of environment to the advertising of the finished product' (p. 13, note). The term 'presentation' has been taken over from the American, and compared with the narrow sense of simply staring at advertising while remaining unaware of its function, this more comprehensive term has its advantages since it emphasizes the moment of display. 'Commodity aesthetics' emphasizes the use of the beautiful illusion alongside the functional determinant. Equally this concept encapsulates human sensuality to which the beautiful illusion appeals and which is thus drawn into this context of investigation.

36   Bongard, *Fetische des Konsums*, p. 25.
37   Helmut Schmidt, 'Die Macht der Information' in *Die Zeit*, 52, 25 December 1970, p. 36.
38   Ibid.
39   Gerhard Voigt, *Zur Kritik der Theorien über die Sprache der Nationalsozialismus* (unpublished thesis, University of Berlin, December, 1970). See especially the appendix on 'Goebbels as a technician of trademarks'.
40   Georg Lukács, *The Destruction of Reason* (London: Merlin, 1980), trans. Peter Palmer, p. 726. See also Voigt, *Zur Kritik der Theorien*.
41   Voigt, *Zur Kritik der Theorien*.
42   For a social-democratic view, see J. Feddersen, 'Politik muß verkauft werden' in *Die Neue Gesellschaft*, V (1958), p. 21–6.
43   Wilhelm Alff, *Der Begriff des Faschismus und andere Aufsätze zur Zeitgeschichte* (Frankfurt: 1971), p. 23 f, note 17.
44   Gert Mattenklott, *Bilderdienst. Ästhetische Opposition bei Beardsley und George* (Munich: 1970), p. 116.
45   H. L. Blies, 'Die Ausstrahlung des Werbegeschenkes' in *Industriekurier*, 30 April 1970, a special issue entitled 'Mit Geschenken werben'.
46   According to 'Werbegeschenke als Kontaktmittel', *FAZ*, 2 September 1971, p. 17. Ernst Gotta of the general partnership

of Ludwig Gotta leather goods, who is the manufacturer quoted here, started up production under the name 'Gottapac' in an area which, Gotta says, 'has recently undergone a rapid increase'. His idea was to introduce 'packagings with a so-called secondary use, i.e. little boxes and cases in a variety of forms for spirits, coffee, tea or sweets, tobacco, cosmetics and toys. After the product itself has been used up, the packages can be used by the buyer for other things.' (*FAZ*, 2 September 1971). The buyer, who has paid for all this at a price, is attracted into buying by the illusion that he is being given something extra.

47 Ibid. Gotta's products, according to *FAZ* 'adorn the most elegant boutiques'. 'On average, the articles, which are given to favoured business associates by companies, cost between DM25 and DM30. Of course at Christmas people are prepared to spend more.' A company's internal hierarchy, as in the macrocosm of capital, gives rise to a corresponding hierarchy of promotional gifts. Eventually this technique finds favour in the innermost recesses of the company. With such 'gifts' capital encourages additional loyalty to the firm and even harder work.

48 *Blick durch die Wirtschaft*, 1 September 1971.

49 Ibid. Felicitas' turnover in 1970 was DM4.5 million. The company expanded 'its range of offers by further services: the gift service "Mother and Child", as well as the Felicitas Sales Promotion Service. This expansion also includes the Felicitas Driving School, where all learner-drivers receive a gift from their instructor as a reward for passing the test.' In order to avoid at all cost the expense of personal delivery and to achieve more effective distribution, new techniques have recently been developed, wherein trial packets of the commodity are attached by some synthetic adhesive directly on to the appropriate advertising hand-out. Cosmetics in particular are distributed in this way. While a small part of the actual commodity remains attached to its colourful appearance as it flies off disembodied into the world, every effort is made to ensure that it also retains a small element of the needs of those people it is intended for. (cf. 'Duftende Anzeigen' *Blick durch die Wirtschaft*, 22 September 1971, p. 1).

50   Horst Zimmermann, 'Bewußtseinsstörung im Selbstbedienung-
      sladen. Lockendes Angebot und persönliche Konflikte als
      häufigste Ursache für Ladendiebstähle' in *Der Tagesspiegel*,
      25 July 1971. See further quotations from the Karstadt Con-
      ference in Siegen on shop-lifting. See also the categorical but
      confusingly written article by Elisabeth Trunk, 'Tempel der
      Versuchung. Diebstähle in Kaufhäusern', *Frankfurter Rund-
      schau*, 4 September 1971, p. 11. By contrast with the bour-
      geois right-wing *Tagesspiegel*, this liberal paper enthusiastically
      takes up the campaign against shop-lifters after the author
      herself has had a go at shop-lifting – with the cooperation of
      the particular department store, of course – in order to
      demonstrate the ineffectiveness of the store detectives, and
      thus to indicate the seriousness of the matter. The article lays
      the responsibility not at the door of the commodities' styling
      but with their completion and the unstable disposition – if not
      'left-wing ideology' – of the perpetrator. It tacitly ignores the
      social relations which lie at the root of the buyer's relationship
      with the world of commodities. Is the perpetrator, the author
      asks, 'a routine criminal type, or an unstable person who can-
      not hold out in the face of the enormous temptation an excess(!)
      of commodities presents?' In reality the tension between a feel-
      ing of inadequacy and this excess affords the perpetrator much
      in the way of promising appearances.

51   Even in Trunk's article 'Tempel der Versuchung', which other-
      wise completely covers up social relations, we are given a
      glimpse into the relationship between commodity aesthetics
      and shop-lifting:

> Commodities are arranged in such a sophisticated way to
> encourage the impulse to grab something, that hardly any
> customer can pass by directly. 'The commodity must be
> presented in such a way that the customer would like to steal it,'
> commented one window-dresser and this in effect forces the
> deliberate arousal of impulse-buying two steps further on, past
> the compulsion to buy and on to the compulsion to pilfer. Now
> the customer is playing with fire . . .

The continuation of the sentence would not be out of place in a
manual on how to cobble together sentences, for quick as a

flash the author changes level and standpoint. Now she is no longer talking about the context of effects, but skips easily into the camouflage required by capital, which would like to see the machinery of prosecution safely in the hands of the police if not justice itself, basically well out of the public eye:

> Now the customer is playing with fire, a game which serious representatives of the store do not go along with. For them the shop-lifter is the criminal, who must answer for their crimes before the bench.

Thus it is not their advertising that these serious representatives do not go along with, but any acquittal for the victims of their advertising successes.

52 *Klau mich* ('Grab me'), a book-title from the First Commune imitates this ambivalence. However, since the title is formulated only from the stealing aspect in its ambivalent call, taken from commodity aesthetics, to possess the commodity, it does not so much shed light on the relations involved as perform the task of an advertisement itself. 'Grab me' works as a particularly intense form of 'buy me'.

53 Baran and Sweezy, *Monopoly Capital*, p. 131.

54 For the individual techniques for regenerating demand by artificial ageing, system variation, complementary products and general 'design' alterations, cf. Chup Friemert, 'Design und Gesellschaft', in *Funktionen bildender Kunst in unserer Gesellschaft* edited by the Working Group for Basic Research in the NGBK (Berlin: 1970; 2nd ed. 1971).

55 See the letter from veterinary director, Dr. Lübke of Zehlendorf, Berlin in *Test*, 10 (1971); and also in this issue photographs of cross-sections of these three containers.

56 Kulischer, *Allgemeine Wirtschaftsgeschichte*, vol. II, p. 147. Kulischer quotes the directive as mentioned in Bein, *Die Industrie des sächsischen Voigtlandes*, vol. II, *Textilindustrie*, 1886, p. 536.

57 *Die Welt*, 26 May 1970.

58 *Der Spiegel*, 49 (1967). The following extracts are also from this source.

59 The shoe industry has not been lagging behind in all this.

Supported by periodic aesthetic innovation and differentiation, it moved into men's shoes (see chapter four, section 5
on the lyric poetry of advertising, in the present work) and
advertised thus: 'Old shoes make you look poverty-striken!'
From this slogan there followed plans of campaign which
emphasize the terrorist tendencies of this propaganda: 'Men,
get rid of those shabby old shoes. There's plenty of room in
the wardrobe for new ones! Every suit deserves new, matching
shoes. You can afford new shoes, but you can't afford to be
seen in old ones.' (e.g. in *Stern*, 39 (1970), p. 164).

60   The world's largest producer of 'pre-packed foods' – the
Kraft corporation – which managed a turnover of 2.75 thousand million dollars in 1970, operates through permanent
innovation. 'At the end of 1969, 57% of the company's 400 or
so articles in turnover was taken up with products that had
only appeared on the market in the last ten years.' If not the
articles themselves then their appearance, name and form of
packaging, not forgetting the increase in price relative to use-
value, were all innovatory (cf. 'Wachstum durch Neuheiten',
Tagesspiegel, 1 October 1971, p. 25).

Chapter Two

1   Plato's Republic in *The Dialogues of Plato*, trans. B. Jowett
4th ed. (Oxford: Clarendon Press, 1953), vol. II, p. 376.
2   'Putabo . . . cunctaque externa nihil aliud esse quam ludifica-
tiones somniorum, quibus insidias credulitati meae tetendit:
considerabo meipsum tanquam manus non habentem, non
oculos, non carnem, non sanguinem, non aliquem sensum'
(Descartes 'Meditatio Prima' in *Meditationes De Prima
Philosophia*, Amsterdam: 1642) p. 13 f.
3   Ibid., p. 24: 'Nisi iam forte respexissem ex fenestra homines
in platea transeuntes, quos etiam ipsos non minus usitate
quam ceram dico me videre: quid autem video praeter pileos &
vestes, sub quibus latere possent automata.'
4   See Descartes' second meditation, *Meditationes*, p. 23.
5   The fact that an object's mere appearance can be detached and
used for purposes of deception is so acceptable to bourgeois

jurisdiction that it refuses to prosecute photocopying offences even in the area of forgery. According to a ruling in the first Federal Criminal Court, in Germany a photocopy cannot have the basic characteristics of a document and thus its forgery cannot constitute a documentary forgery. The proof given was that a document is 'the embodiment of a declaration', a piece of evidence in itself which reveals its author, while a photocopy produces only a 'more or less faithful duplicate' which, like a written copy, is a mere reproduction presented as the embodiment of a declaration, but which unlike a written copy is pictorial (cf. 'Fotokopien gelten nicht als Urkunden', *Tagesspiegel*, 13 October 1971). In the right of ownership, bourgeois law defends through the claims of the embodied appearance its own claims to private property, which conversely generates the systematic disembodiment of the appearance of things in commodity production.

6   Even polished, shiny or transparent surfaces are sold as calculated methods of creating an illusion in the packaging market, which is also an advertising market. 'Almost any object,' the tin-foil manufacturer, Forchheim GmbH advertised in 1964, 'becomes a winner when wrapped in tin-foil: such an attractive face cannot fail to promote sales.' A special issue of foil 'is especially suited to wrap chocolates, biscuit and cigarette boxes and is excellent too for wrapping up different articles as special offers . . . its shiny surface is a sure-fire sales success.' (Advertisement in *Der Spiegel*, 6 May 1964, p. 77 and in the edition of 1 April 1964).

7   One of the forms in which the colourful appearance of commodities is circulated belongs to the distribution method of the mail-order company, namely the mail-order catalogue. The firm 'Quelle' alone calculates around DM130 in catalogue costs (cf. 'Der Katalog enthält 40,000 Artikel', *Tagesspiegel*, 19 September 1971, p. 12). These costs cover a huge outlay in technical equipment and personnel.

> For around seven months two hundred graphics experts, copywriters, photographers, designers and managerial staff have been busy preparing the catalogue with more than seven-hundred pages. Seventy-six photographic models posed for the

catalogue in Majorca, on the Zugspitze, in Frankfurt and in Scotland. But of a correspondingly huge number of shots, exactly 10,001 photos had to be selected, and twelve major printers used 8,500 tonnes of paper and 560 tonnes of ink in the four or five weeks it took to print them.' (*FAZ*, 10 August 1971)

No actual commodity-body can actually keep up with the overwhelming technical perfection that stage-manages and reproduces its appearance in this way.

8   *Die Erzählungen aus den tausendundein Nächten* (Wiesbaden: 1953), trans. Enno Littmann, vol. IV, p. 233–55.

9   If the principle of domination usually suppresses and often almost wipes out traditions and customs by its helpful service, nevertheless recurring moments arise in which even the profiteering agent of capitalism ponders the passing of the years with a certain melancholy and hankers after the good old days. When the Oetker company introduced a new brand of lager on to the market, after four years spent developing its image, an economic correspondent at the *FAZ* noted: 'Once again we're made to see clearly what sort of a world we live in. Today a lager has been sketched out on the drawing-board and 'constructed' like a washing powder or a radio. Gone are the days when hearty brewers produced nothing but barley-wine in the manner of their forefathers. If you order a lager these days, you'll get a standardized brand-name. In this melancholy mood', the correspondent concludes, 'let's raise our glasses and drink to the old days of brewing when lager was just lager and nothing else.' (*FAZ*, 8 September 1971). While developing the 'Prinz Pilsener', the 'national trade-mark' of the Oetker group, laboratory tests were concentrating from the outset on a product they called 'Marketing-Mix', which expresses the wish that the actual liquid commodity-body should be constructed from the point of view of its becoming a 'hit' and advertising campaigns. Now that the *Frankfurter Allgemeine*'s correspondent has once again realized what sort of a world he lives in, and he's drowned his sorrows with a pint of 'Marketing-Mix', he can get back to his daily journalistic practice of – if we may pass judgement on the *FAZ*'s journalism – systematic mystification to secure the domination by big-business

capital in this world, a practice which should justifiably cause
the occasional bout of melancholy on a mass scale.

10 Bertolt Brecht, *Das Badener Lehrstück vom Einverständnis* in
Gesammelte Werke (Frankfurt: Suhrkamp, 1967), vol. I,
pp. 593–98.

11 See Sigmund Freud, *Introductory Lectures on Psychoanalysis*
(Harmondsworth: Penguin, 1973, repr. 1984), The Pelican
Freud Library, p. 452. Here, Freud speaks of anxiety as 'the
universally current coinage for which *any* effective impulse is
or can be exchanged.'

12 A statement on the politics of the publishing house Burda,
whose owner is politically on the right wing of the Christian
Democrats (CDU/CSU), confirmed my thesis soon after it was
first published. The thesis, in brief, is as follows: sexuality in
the service of commodity aesthetics remains contradictory; the
dialectic of the capitalist domination based on offers has not
been laid to rest. On 26 June 1970, Burda announced that its
men's magazine, *M*, would be immediately discontinued, giving as a reason, that since the launch of the magazine one year
previously, changes had occurred in the market. The general
sexualizing of the magazine market would have forced the
editorial board into the sort of competition considered incompatible with the style of the publishing house, just to keep the
magazine going financially. However this confirmation of the
arbitrariness of these purposely liberated instincts must be
appreciated cautiously from at least two aspects. First, the
commercial difficulties must have already been considerable
for the 'style of the publishing house' to be no longer a matter
of business, but instead the guardian of the nation's morality.
Secondly, and this is just the other side of the coin, the interest
in freedom of sexual matters must be considered as only very
weak and subject to continual ambivalence; although this is
not to say that someday the balance, now weighted heavily
towards profit-making, should not tip in favour of freedom
just for once.

Chapter Three

1   Werner Sombart, *Der moderne Kapitalismus*, vol. II/1, p. 464.
2   Mandeville, *The Fable of the Bees*, p. 215 f. My attention was drawn to this scene by H-O. Riethus.
3   Peter Jessen, 'Der mißtrauische Kunde. Wie man ihn erkennt und wie man mit ihm umgeht', in *Außendienst-Informationen, Schriftlicher und programmierter Trainingskurs für Verkäufer*, edited by Norbert Müller (Munich), no.48.
4   Wolfgang Menge, *Der verkaufte Käufer. Die Manipulation der Konsumgesellschaft* (Vienna 1971), p. 334.
5   Quotations taken from Menge, pp. 334 and 336. Menge manages to present the system of sales-talk accurately in his book, as the material he is working with is almost crying out to be analysed. For nothing comes across more clearly than technical instructions on how systematically to obfuscate both language and consciousness. Apart from this, Menge's book lacks any theoretical analysis and completely falls victim to the system whose ubiquitous forms of appearance he is complaining about and which might even valorize his protest: this is indicated in the sub-title's use of the ideological term 'consumer society'. This book could quite easily be accepted on to the list of books that appear in the *Deutsche National–und Soldatenzeitung* as rewards for finding new subscribers.
6   Menge, *Der verkaufte Käufer,* p. 344.
7   The adverts with which Cologne's *Werbegemeinschaft Bistumspresse* advertises for advertisers have the advantage of using uncommonly clear language. What is more, in this respect they have an advantage over the pages of the Diocesan Press itself. 'The Press's readers are in the main Catholic, obviously. But what else are they?' Under this flashy headline reads the answer: 'Well, hard-working consumers, for example – mother, the happy consumer; father, the willing consumer; teenagers, blissful consumers' and this supreme happiness along with their spiritual fulfilment is put on sale by the Diocesan Press which draws up these calculations for potential advertisers: 'According to an opinion poll, 82 per cent of all

readers of the Diocesan Press have more trust in that paper than in their daily newspaper! The Diocesan Press is a good medium for advertising that requires trust!' (*Werben-Verkaufen*, 28, 1969). A previous advert in the Press explained this spiritual trust that is on sale: 'Everybody trusts the Diocesan Press. It has a higher reader-intensity, and provides infinite trustworthiness, from which advertising can profit. Yes, there is no better place to reach your audience than through this honest advertising medium' (*Werben-Verkaufen*, 18, 1968).

These Evangelists are all too generous in their sale of blessedness. No indictment could expose the relations involved more sharply than the Press's own advertising does. 'The reasoning comes full circle: place your announcements between words from the Bible, your advertisements between articles of contemplation. Unhesitatingly, the reader will transfer his trust from one to the other!' So went an advert in 'The most widely-read evangelical Sunday paper in the Rhineland', *Der Weg* (*ZV + ZV*, 16, 1968). Similar adverts in *bravo*, *Neue Welt*, *Eltern*, and many others, recommend to their readers the specifically stimulating effect that their editorial section can have. The subject-matter of privately owned mass media may differ greatly, but in the competition for advertising they can all be reduced to the one common denominator – profit. My attention was drawn to the examples from *Werben verkaufen* and *ZV + ZV* by a Christian Gellner film, which was made as a project by the class in Information Graphics at the erstwhile Academy of Graphic Art, Printing and Advertising in West Berlin.

8 Among trading nations, the rhetorical training in sales-talk informs and moulds the national culture in general to the extent that members of such nations may be identified by those in other societies who possess related skills.

9 Rhetoric, alongside production and selling under capital, has become subordinated to the division of labour, taking its place in society as sales-talk. Selling becomes a particular vocation and one's ability to sell sums up a person's characteristics. As the reproduction of the class relations between capital and wage-labour expands, it becomes apparent that relatively fewer

people have something to say. Orders and information, which are now the dominant forms, do not constitute a conversation. The private buyer, walking up the commodity-aesthetic aisles of the supermarket, is not actually doing anything except buying or not buying, remaining silent, albeit deeply moved. With their mouth watering at the commodity-stimulus on the shelves, the buyer swallows any mistrust and suppresses it inside. Occasionally the broad social disappearance of the rhetorical and conversational arts is put down to the advent of radio, films and television. However, one only needs to meet a company representative, a carpet or door-to-door salesman, whose rhetorical abilities are way above the general level, to realize that a simple psychological reason is too superficial. In a political context, speaking abilities are once again of central importance, for if the masses are politically mobilized then changes in speaking abilities can come about on a mass scale. In its objective social function at the moment, speaking abilities will either waste away altogether or be developed once again.

10   Bertolt Brecht, *Der Tui-Roman* in Gesammelte Werke, vol. V, p. 674–5.

11   Ibid., p. 678.

12   Siegfried Kracauer, *Schriften* (Frankfurt, 1971), vol. I, pp. 222–4. The following quotations are also from these pages.

13   There is of course another functional area apart from this one, an area which is only mediatedly linked to the personification of the sales function, namely the connection between the aesthetic innovation of open-plan office landscapes and fashionable innovations in the appearance of office employees. The following extract from a report in *Blick durch die Wirtschaft* (6 November 1971, p. 1) shows that the agents of capital are very much aware of and happy to make use of this connection, even to the extent of consciously aiming at it:

> On the occasion of a press symposium, Dr Schmithals, a member of the executive board of Hoesch Hohenlimburg-Schwerte AG, commented on a particularly pleasing side-effect of the new open-plan office landscapes. This, he said, had caused

a noticeable effort among female employees to appear as
fashionably dressed as possible, since they were suddenly no
longer sitting in a quiet little office somewhere, but were arranged
on the silver salver of the open-plan office. Two days after the
employees were installed in the new open-plan office, almost all
the female employees in quick succession appeared in new,
more fashionable outfits. This is, however, not to say that there
aren't still the open-plan office sulks who go around all day
with their scarves on. Nevertheless, the variety of colourful steel
furniture in an open-plan office, luxurious foliage, partitions,
and consultation rooms with a small refreshment bar maintains
the impression of a 'happy' office landscape.

14 Bertolt Brecht, 'Der Dreigroschenprozeß', *Schriften zur
Literatur und Kunst* in Gesammelte Werke, vol. VIII, p. 164.
15 Ibid., p. 163.
16 The following information comes from the *Frankfurter Rundschau,* 6 December 1969.
17 Bertolt Brecht, 'The Seven Deadly Sins of the Petty
Bourgeoisie' in *Bertolt Brecht Collected Plays*, edited by John
Willett and Ralph Manheim (London: Eyre Methuen, 1979),
vol. II, part 3, scene 7, p. 82.
18 Kracauer mentions in his study of employees at the end of
the twenties, years in which lighting techniques in the sales
area had been greatly developed, the 'beneficial influence'
– beneficial as far as capital is concerned – 'that lighting has
on both the desire to buy and on sales assistants . . . the light
dazzles rather than illuminates . . . and thus the illusion is
preserved' (*Schriften*, p. 284).
19 *Frankfurter Rundschau*, 26 February 1970. According to this
same source the sales area in retail shops in the Federal
Republic increased from 23 million to 32 million square metres
between 1960 and 1970. Thus according to these figures, the
investment in salesrooms costs around DM4 thousand million
a year (1970). According to more recent figures on the other
hand, 1970 saw a DM3.6 thousand million (5 per cent) drop in
investment in comparison with retail trade in the previous
year. But according to an Ifo survey, 1971 will enter a period
of investment of at least 10 per cent increase. 'This growth in
investment should chiefly be borne by the larger retail outlets,

which register a yearly turnover of over DM10 million' (*FAZ*, 13 August 1971).

20   *Der Tagesspiegel*, 24 February 1970.

21   Quoted in *Der Tagesspiegel*, 24 February 1970.

22   'Das Warenhaus als Erlebnisbühne. Nachbemerkungen zum Fall Globus' by J. Jürgen Jeske, *FAZ*, 4 August 1971. Other quotations and information on 'Globus' are also from this source.

23   The extensive aesthetic innovation in department stores which followed the success of boutiques occurred in the same year (1967) in which even men's fashion came under pressure from economic crisis and declining turnover. It gave itself a boost of aesthetic innovation, following a sideways glance at the growing number of boutiques which sell imported commodities (see Chapter one, section 7) 'The second effect of monopolization – aesthetic innovation' in the present work).

24   *FAZ*, 2 September 1971, p. 15. This also mentions the story of the legendary pioneer in the world of commodities – the Wertheim store which was completed in 1927 in Leipzig Square.

> Its ground floor was more than double the size of the Reichstag's ground floor . . . The building, erected by Professor Messel, was richly decorated with sculptures and bronze reliefs by famous sculptors. Its interior was covered in marble inlay-work, and silver-plated terracotta pieces were on display. The carpet department was panelled in Italian walnut and in the numerous inner courtyards, fountains worked in Istrian limestone were playing.

25   Ibid.

26   *FAZ*, 20 August 1971, p. 15.

27   Ibid.

28   *Der Tagesspiegel*, 24 February 1970.

29   A new name has already been coined for the new stage-management of the sales-area and the whole sales-experience: 'Amusement Store' (*Der Tagesspiegel*, 24 February 1970). Coining new names is a standard component in the process of carrying out innovations and thus devaluing a portion of the retail invested capital.

30 *Der Tagesspiegel*, 24 February 1970.

31 Ka-De-We advertisement in *Der Tagesspiegel*, 17 October 1971.

32 Taken from Heidrun Abromeit, *Das Politische in der Werbung. Wahlwerbung und Wirtschaftswerbung in der Bundesrepublik* (Opladen: Westdeutscher Verlag GmbH, 1972), p. 138. Brecht provides a further example in the *Threepenny Novel*: Peachum sells packaging to beggars, which they in turn can use to 'sell' their own wretched existences on the streets. (Harmondsworth: Penguin, 1961), pp. 19–21. In effect he sells the kind of appearance that will appeal to people's hearts.

33 *Twen*, 12 (1969), p. 16 f; taken from Doris and Thomas von Freyberg, *Kritik der Sexualerziehung* (Frankfurt: 1971), p. 124.

34 Marlies Nehrstede, 'Den modischen Geschmack der Normalverbraucherin bestimmen hauptsächlich die Zeitschriften', *Frankfurter Rundschau*, 13 September 1971.

35 Ibid: 'Weiß is by no means unhappy with this trend' – which is in effect a form of prostitution, fashionable clothes serving to package the body like a commodity – 'It means that his female customers want a completely new wardrobe from head to toe at least every six weeks, and this increases turnover.'

36 According to *FAZ*, 30 July 1971.

37 An interim balance produced by a market research institute and commissioned by the company came up with this report on their success: Questions to engaged and recently married women showed that 29 per cent possess a diamond engagement ring, 12 per cent a triple set (pair of wedding rings and matching diamond ring) and that, moreover, 6 per cent were expecting a triple set 'at any rate' on getting married, and 21 per cent were 'counting on' receiving one.

38 'Sind Diamanten wirklich eine gute Geldanlage?', *Blick durch die Wirtschaft*, 20 September 1971, p. 1.

39 In a report given on the occasion of preparations for the Sixth German National Precious Stones Day, an increase in turnover of 15 per cent was recorded regarding jewellers in the Federal Republic in the first nine months of 1971. Further information confirms the trend that De Beers is exploiting: 'The growth can be noticed particularly in small stones of 0.10 to 0.30 carats . . .

A noticeable shift has been discerned in those buying stones. As a result of the world-wide inflationary trend, jewellers are profiting increasingly from the association of jewellery with investment.' (*Der Tagesspiegel*, 21 September 1971). In this case, many people will have to make do with advertising slogans.

40 'Sind Diamanten wirklich eine gute Geldanlage?'

41 Dorothee Backhaus, 'Madames Gesicht wird bunt bemalt. Natürlichkeit nicht mehr gefragt . . .', *Frankfurter Rundschau*, 31 July 1971.

42 Ibid.

43 *Der Spiegel*, 10, (1968), p. 78 f. Between 1960 and 1967 the turnover had more than doubled.

44 According to the *Frankfurter Rundschau* (12 December 1968), production value in the cosmetics industry increased by 16 per cent in the first half of 1968 by comparison with the same period in 1967. If the VAT figures are removed from 1967, then the growth becomes 22 per cent. The German company Holiday Magic Kosmetik Aschaffenburg, which trades in exclusively important commodities, declared its trade margin to be 65 per cent of its retail price – which corresponds to scarcely 200 per cent of the import company's cost price. All this does not yet take production costs into account (cf. *Frankfurter Rundschau*, 15 September 1971). Chemist shops in particular are profiting from the growth in this area – in 1970 their turnover increased by 7 per cent. This increase was, however, achieved by a 0.8 per cent reduction in the number of chemist shops. The drop in numbers, according to Heinrich Gewand, a Christian Democrat and President of the Federation of German Pharmacists, corresponded with the general reduction in the number of retail shops, a reduction, he claimed, of 2.5–3 per cent in 1970: 'in recent years', he remarked, 'they have become unusually scarce.' (*Frankfurter Rundschau*, 18 September 1971).

45 Retail turnover in hair-care products was DM830 million in 1967 (*Der Spiegel*, 10, 1968). In the first six months of 1968 'production value' in these products came to DM250 million (14 per cent more than in the same period in 1967) (*Frankfurter Rundschau*, 12 December 1968).

46 'New products', an executive board member of Pond's, informed us recently in Munich, 'should ensure further expansion' (*FAZ*, 14 August 1971). In the first six months of 1968 an above-average growth appeared in a specific area of hair-care products – 'sprays, creams and setting lotions' – a growth of about 20 per cent compared with 14 per cent in the group as a whole (*Frankfurter Rundschau*, 12 December 1968). The group with the most noticeable growth is characterized by products which are either technically new (e.g. hair sprays) or are only recently produced for a mass-market.

47 According to *Der Spiegel*, 10 (1968).

48 *FAZ*, 13 August 1971.

49 *FAZ*, 'Lebensglück mit Kosmetik', 14 August 1971.

50 According to *Der Spiegel*, 10, (1968). In 1967, DM80 million worth of perfumes for men were sold.

51 Ibid., quoting Ernest Dichter. The following quotations are also taken from this source.

52 *FAZ*, 13 August 1971. In 1970 cosmetics for men still only constituted 10 per cent of Rubinstein's European turnover. The lion's share of women's cosmetics in Europe is made up of 'treatment' products (scarcely 50 per cent) and make-up itself (35 per cent).

53 Sütex has 850 subsidiary outlets which altogether have a retail turnover of DM1.1 thousand million. Of these subsidiaries 100–150 are more or less purely menswear shops. See also *FAZ*, 18 August 1971.

54 'Atomic Fashions' of Düsseldorf is a subsidiary enterprise of 'Tailordress' in Chur. In this area it was regarded as a 'second outlet' for the Ahlers group, one of the largest German clothing manufacturers, employing 5,000–6,000 people. The Ahlers family owns 25 per cent of the shares in 'Tailordress'. See also *FAZ*, 18 and 19 August and 6 September 1971.

55 *FAZ*, 18 August 1971. Until the cooperation agreement came to an end, its net encompassed 65 centres and depots of 'independent' retail shops. In order to win over retailers, the company provides them with shop-fittings as well as helping with rent as part of the leasing procedures. Moreover, the retailers are offered an increase in window-dressing and advertising

services, as well as courses in selling and management (cf. *FAZ*, 6 September 1971).

56   The following quotations are taken from an advert placed by the Karstadt company in *Tagesspiegel*, 9 December 1969, which is typical of the propaganda used to sell innovations in the pullover trade.

57   For 'no eunuch flatters his despot more basely or uses more infamous means to revive his flagging capacity for pleasure, in order to win a surreptitious pleasure for himself, than does the eunuch of industry . . . in order to . . . coax the gold from the pocket of his dearly beloved neighbour.' (Marx, 'Economic and Philosophical Manuscripts', p. 359).

58   The pullover advert also promotes two other commodities: boots 'in the style of a revolutionary' and 'Arden for Men'. Youth fetishism and aestheticized power are thus combined in a new image.

59   Karstadt advert in, *inter alia, Tagesspiegel*, 24 September 1971.

60   *Der Spiegel*, 14 September 1970.

61   The advertisement of this brand name of men's underwear did not just use the 'men fit' slogan of Schiesser which presented the penis in the form of a sheath, but it also moved the naked male, back and side view, onto the scene. Since the beginning of May 1967, Sélimaille ('Ceinture noire') has advertised in France using nude photos of Frank Protopapa, who was famous world-wide as the first publicly displayed male nude. The male nude was introduced just as female nudes were appearing on every page. 'As a "stopper",' i.e. an arresting image, 'breasts are indisputably in top position,' commented an advertising consultant in Munich, Jörg Nimmergut. However, the 'libido-appeal' (Nimmergut) of nude advertising threatened to disappear amid the nude photos which were appearing in the editorial section of magazines. 'Advertising's strategic response was the naked male . . . half-naked men entice us to buy Ronson cigarette lighters and Prestige perfumes. In France a full-nude has already appeared – albeit rather out of focus and necessarily at a distance – advertising Pierre Cardin perfume for men' (see *Der Spiegel*, 24, 1967, p. 118). Protopapa's nude photos were shot at close-up and printed sharply: what his nudity revealed most, however, was

capital's efforts at profit-making in a particular competitive situation. Now, for once, male nudity had turned up and had gained entry – if only as a back-view at first – into the editorial section of magazines, into the theatre and films. One of the fundamental socio-sexual role-differences between men and women, which was determined by bourgeois society, is the fixing of woman as the sexual object and man as the sexual subject; and here it was beginning – if only on the level of a symptom – to even out.

62 Under cover of this development moves were being made to push back the frontiers of what could be published. 'For the first time in 1970 a consumers' advertising campaign was launched in the magazines *Eltern, Jasmin, M, Spiegel* and *bravo*, against resistance in the media generally to the advertising of London brand condoms.' Overcoming this resistance, which had cost the firm a considerable sum of money, paid for itself by producing an even more considerable sum. 'With an increase in turnover of over 18 per cent and "a profit increase out of all proportion by comparison", the financial year 1970/71 (31.3.) was "by far the best" year the company had ever had' (*Blick durch die Wirtschaft*, 21 October 1971).

63 See *Der Spiegel*, 22 (1971), p. 190, wherein the advertising photo is copied.

64 See the section on 'Ästhetizimus und Warenästhetik', in W. F. Haug, 'Warenästhetik und Angst', *Das Argument*, 28 (1964) 4th ed., 1970, p. 15.

65 See Marx 'Economic and Philosophical Manuscripts', p. 362.

66 Kinney Music Gmbh, Hamburg, one of the numerous national subsidiaries of the American holdings company, Kinney National Service. 'The founding company in this hybrid firm forms a trans-regional organization of cleaning agencies, a network of parking-lots and a chain of funeral directors. Added to this was an involvement in the world of magazines, i.e. the marketing firm Periodical Publications. From among these interests a magazine appeared and the copyright on comic characters such as Superman and Batman was won. In 1968 the most major advance in the entertainments market occurred with the acquisition of Warner Brothers. This group had early on expanded their firm production and studios by starting up

a record industry, to which Warner Brothers music publishers also belongs. It controls the copyright on Gershwin's music amongst others. The Warner group record industry operates independently as 'Reprise Records' (formerly belonging to Frank Sinatra), 'Atlantic' and 'Elektra' (*FAZ*, 21 August 1971).

67 The record in question is 'Sticky Fingers' by the Rolling Stones; see also *Der Spiegel*, 22 (1971), p. 154.

68 Kracauer, 'Die Angestellten', in *Schriften*, p. 247 f.

69 Bertolt Brecht, 'The Seven Deadly Sins of the Petty Bour-geoisie,' in *Collected Plays*, vol. II, part 3, scene 7, p. 82.

70 Ibid., p. 246.

71 Ibid., p. 248. see also chapter four, section 4 of the present work, 'Collective praxis and the illusion industry under capitalism'.

72 In a questionnaire from the Contest Institute, which was pub-lished 'in a preliminary report to the International Fashion Con-ference in Cologne in 1972' (see *Blick durch die Wirtschaft*, 16 October 1971), 54 per cent of men over 30 answered

> that in their families they frequently discussed fashion with the younger members. Moreover, one man in four was particularly interested in hearing the younger generation's opinion on these matters . . . 27% of men over 30 possess clothes which were bought either when accompanied by a younger person or on the recommendation of a younger person. Frequently these clothes were bought specifically because something similar had been seen to look attractive on a younger person.

Correspondingly the fraction of the complete turnover in men's and boys' clothes known as leisure wear has become increasingly larger: in the case of some 'important manufac-turers in this area' it counts for around 60 per cent.

73 Even the efforts of Agfa to get at the 'money in blue-jeans' by developing a camera and accessories case for young people and thus capturing the market in good time, appear to have merely increased the tendency to fetishize youth. To begin with they covered cameras in denim material, so that their appearance would match the money in a jeans' pocket. However, this calculation did not work, since ideas of technical equipment

are still associated with taking photographs. Then, 'the hottest case in Europe' was tailor-made for young people alongside 'jeans with hooks' to hang them on. Since young people associate expressions like 'taking photographs' with old people, these phrases were replaced in the advertisements with expressions like 'making pictures'. All through the sales campaign, photographic shop assistants had to wear jeans, until finally, after initial difficulties, the commodity was bought – but by adults. (cf. also Menge, *Der verkaufte Käufer*, p. 242 f).

74 Supplement in, *inter alia, Der Tagesspiegel*, 30 December 1970.

75 Supplement in *Der Tagesspiegel*, 3 January 1971. A catalogue from *Musterring* included some months later in the same newspaper blatantly links aesthetic innovation with general mobility and playfulness in a socio-sexual sense. 'Mobility is the name of the game', 'Mobility means variation, combination, experimentation', 'Action for living is everything', 'Today this way and tomorrow the same, but the day after it's different, as for example. . . .' Every which-way is just another example, a given number from an endless line of other numbers. Thus in these continually changing options of sensuality capital creates a mirror-image of its own movements.

76 See *Blick durch die Wirtschaft* 7 September 1971, p. 5: 'Now hope for the bedroom. German carpets still have a chance of major growth – a branch report.' Carpet consumption in the Federal Republic in terms of square metres per person occupies only third position in Europe. Above all 'the bedroom must recover considerably. The symbol of this newly developed quality is animal skins and consequently the industry has developed luxurious shagpile carpets as well as tufted shags, velours and hooked velour carpets, to cater for this area.'

77 Some readers might object to this, saying that such a sexual landscape is better than those old German rooms, moulded out of plastic or like a piece of carved wood, which 'represents' a fine example – of reactionary architecture for authoritarian people. The analysis is not inveighing against sexuality, but as best it can against capital, the pimp in this transaction. It is a question of analysing which mechanisms capital's valorization

process, as well as its waste-product, uses to mould human sensuality in a particular way.

78   Peter von Riedt, 'Ein Hund mit traurigen Augen und Schlappohren', *FAZ*, 14 August 1971, p. 17. The other information on 'Hush Puppies' is also taken from this source.

79   Ibid.

80   Ibid.

81   'To some extent the needs and wants of people have to be continuously stirred up.' Ernest Dichter, *The Strategy of Desire* (London: Boardman, 1960) p. 265. (Quoted in Abromeit, *Das Politische in der Werbung*, p. 180).

82   Bertolt Brecht, 'The Rise and Fall of the City of Mahagonny', in *Collected Plays*, vol. II, part 3, scene 11, p. 26.

83   Marx, *Capital*, vol. I, p. 125.

84   When flower-growing becomes a part of capitalism's valorization function you can be sure that behind these powerful natural impulses there are the even more powerful impulses of profiteering and capital competition. In fact the cultivation of flowers played an important economic role in founding one of the first pre-industrial areas of production in developed capitalist countries, in this case in Holland. 'In the 1630s the feverous speculation over the "Great Tulip Scandal" came to a head. The tulip had been brought to Europe from Turkey and had soon become established as the favourite Dutch plant. New, rare and particularly favourite show specimens were bred. Tulips were entered on the stock-market . . . and tulip-bulbs were used as shares which could be speculated on in every possible way. At the height of this speculation, tulip-bulbs became literally worth their weight in gold, until in 1637 the market crashed catastrophically' (see Kulischer, *Allgemeine Wirtschaftsgeschichte*, vol. II, p. 319 f).

85   Marx, *Capital*, vol. I, p. 163.

Chapter Four

1   Marx, *Grundrisse, Foundations of the Critique of Political Economy* (Harmondsworth: Penguin, 1973), p. 287.

2   See Kurt Steinhaus, 'Probleme der Systemauseinandersetzung

im nachfaschistischen Deutschland', in *BRD-DDR, Vergleich der Gesellschaftssysteme* (Cologne: 1971), pp. 402–40.

3 Marx, *Capital* (Harmondsworth: Penguin, 1981) vol. III, p. 745. In the 'Communist Manifesto', secondary exploitation is described, without being conceptualized as such, by comparison with the basic exploitation that lies at the heart of the capitalist production process: 'No sooner is the exploitation of the labourer by the manufacturer, so far, at an end, and he receives his wages in cash, than he is set upon by the other portions of the bourgeoisie, the landlord, the shopkeeper, the pawnbroker, etc.' Marx and Engels *Collected Works* (London: Lawrence and Wishart, 1976), vol. VI, p. 491.

4 *FAZ*, 6 August 1971.

5 See also the ironic commentary 'Fehl-Anzeige' in *FAZ*'s business section, 2 October 1971. Even here the social content of an advertisement is shown to be an obstacle to the peaceful and orderly operation of capitalism. 'Why has Helga P. left her desk yet again?', the advert asks, and the answer comes, 'Because occasionally she needs fresh supplies of X chocolate.' The commentator seems to adopt the standpoint of capital, but manages to disguise it by saying that it has become increasingly the case 'for 70 years in this country' that 'office colleagues' are forced 'to make up the work' that their absent friends are neglecting. The article concludes, 'Putting forward these of all people to promote a certain brand of chocolate is simply incomprehensible.' The problem of content, however, remains undiscussed. For our purposes it is important to recognize how mechanisms, of a kind of 'independent self-control' in capital, actually function in class-political questions, even in advertising.

6 Since this extract was first published, further developments in this area have occurred in the GDR, in particular the setting up of 'sorting committees'. It is worth pointing out here a report in *FAZ* (27 July 1971, p. 13) in which the efforts of the editorial staff to create misunderstandings and confusion are obvious. Nevertheless we can elicit from the report that a 'more democratic procedure' in textile buying – and thus in the control of the supply – has been institutionalized in the GDR. 'An honorary body, a "sorting committee" is to be set

up in the factories. This committee, [about whose composition *FAZ* does not inform us] should carry the ultimate responsibility as to which commodities will be offered to the consumer.' The *FAZ*, while wasting no words on the implications of this set-up for society, makes quite sure that it seems not only incomprehensible but also undesirable and certain to cause 'confusion' in the future.

7   Bertolt Brecht, 'Der Dreigroschenprozeß. Ein sociologisches Experiment', *Schriften zur Literatur und Kunst* in Gesammelte Werke, vol. VIII, pp. 161–2. Following on from this, highly topical consequences are drawn from Brecht's insight, regarding the artistic representation of reality. Science too needs to draw from this and could benefit from Brecht's conclusions, *mutatis mutandis*, just as much as 'art' in its narrowest sense can.

> Thus there is really 'something to assemble', something 'artificial', and 'established'. Nevertheless, art is really necessary. But the old concept of art as derived from experience must be shed. For whoever deems reality to be what is experienceable in reality, cannot reproduce themselves. For a long time now we have not been able to experience reality in toto . . . You will no longer recognize the fruits by their taste.

8   K. Marx and F. Engels, *The German Ideology, Collected Works* (London: Lawrence and Wishart, 1976), vol. V, p. 48.
9   Marx, *Capital*, vol. I, p. 168.
10   Bertolt Brecht, 'The Seven Deadly Sins of the Petty Bourgeoisie', in *Collected Plays*, vol. II, part 3, scenes 5 and 7, p. 77 and 82 from which the following quotations are taken.
11   Marx, 'Economic and Philosophical Manuscripts', p. 358.
12   The capitalist hosiery manufacturer, Fritz-Karl Schulte, who uses erotic pictures of women's legs and thighs as advertising both on and off the packaging of his commodity, nevertheless does not let himself be led astray by female charms. 'I have an almost erotic relationship,' he is reported to have said, 'with money.' His advertising consultant, Willy Bloess, is said to have added (probably without any knowledge of Brecht's similar formulation in his *Tui-Roman*): 'He thinks more with

his stomach than with his head.' This means that he personifies his capital body and soul and that he has handed over
his senses and instincts – even the erotic ones – to capital (cf.
Der Spiegel, 5, 1971, p. 56).

13 Marx, *Capital*, vol. I, p. 231.
14 Ibid.
15 Marx, *Capital*, vol. I, p. 230.
16 Marx, *Capital*, vol. I, p. 165.
17 'War and war only can set a goal for mass movements on the
largest scale while respecting the traditional property system.'
And: 'Only war makes it possible to mobilize all of today's
technical resources while maintaining the property system.'
(Walter Benjamin, 'The Work of Art in the Age of Mechanical
Reproduction', in *Illuminations*, London: Cape, 1970, p. 243).
For a critique of Benjamin's theory of fascism see chapter
four, section 7 of the present work.
18 The editors of the book *Manipulation – Die staatsmono-
polistische Bewußtseinsindustrie* (East Berlin, second edition,
1969) have adopted the concept of 'culture industry' (p. 333).
Similarly, as the sub-title indicates, they have adopted the term
'consciousness industry' [*Bewußtseinsindustrie*], which is conceptualized as a polemical contrast to the 'culture industry'
and thus cannot simply be used alternatively with the latter
without taking their relationship into account. Nevertheless,
Enzensberger coined the term 'consciousness industry' within
a theory of totalitarianism, which hovers between equating
communism with fascism on the one hand, and socialist with
capitalist 'industrial societies' on the other. In addition, he links
the term with a curious 'concept of non-material exploitation',
which apparently outstrips the usual material exploitation of
the workers (cf. Hans Magnus Enzensberger, *Einzelheiten
I–Bewußtseins-Industrie*, 6th edition, Frankfurt: 1969,
pp. 7–17). In short, these conceptual tools are in need of
critical revision. However, for our present purposes the provisional concept of the illusion industry (also known as the
distraction industry) must suffice.
19 Quoted from Wolfram Schütte, 'Männerliebe und–leben',
Frankfurter Rundschau, 5 December 1968. The article deals
with the film 'Red River'.

20   Jens-Ulrich Davids, 'Das Wildwestromanheft in der Bundesrepublik', *Der Tagesspiegel*, 30 May 1971. The composition of
the books' readership is most instructive: As *Tagesspiegel*
reports, the books are read 'habitually by all levels of society
with only a slight reduction in frequency in the "upper" levels.
The majority of readers are aged between 16 and 20, the second
largest group comprises 11- to 15-year-olds and the third largest
is made up of 21- to 30-year-olds. The pleasure of reading
Westerns declines rapidly after the age of 30.'

21   According to the editors of *Manipulation*, 'imperialist mass
literature has an extraordinary effect on the public' (p. 305).
However, they do not go on to analyse this effect, unless one
counts as analysis catchwords like 'beautiful dreamworld'
(p. 308) or its ability 'to appeal to our baser instincts' (p. 325).
It is all the more regrettable that what the authors emphasize
about this 'pseudo-literature' is that 'it is not a straightforward
case of deception' (p. 311). To be able to counteract the
influence of this effect, we must understand the possibilities
for its operation.

22   'Imperialist mass culture submits to people's illusions, creating
in its oeuvre a "second reality", a world of illusions purged of
social contradictions,' it generates 'social illusions' (*Manipulation*, p. 331). It is in this sense that I discuss 'illusory solutions' and the 'illusion industry'. But more than this, I am
trying to track down the nature and operation of these illusions.
By calling the energy used up in these illusions a potentially
socialist force, we can discover a possible way into interpreting
the works produced by the illusion industry: amid the most
powerful 'hits', these works encourage us to conceive of them
as illusionary and displaced substitutes for socialism. Such an
interpretation means that the mystery of these mass-effects is
transcended, and criticism can be directed at its illusory and
substitute character. Such a method may be termed a 'hermen-
eutic of determined negation' since it does not simply reject
critical interpretation, but forges links with the illusion's effective content and turns its attention to its practical realization.

23   See the extensive information on p. 160–161 of the present
work, chapter three, note 7.

24   Quoted from Wilhelm Genazino, 'Lyrik, wo niemand sie

vermutet. Die Literatursprache in der Werbung und das Selbst-verständnis der Dichter', *FAZ*, 23 July 1971, p. 24.

25 Dieter Wellershoff, quoted in Genazino, 'Lyrik, wo niemand sie vermutet'.

26 Ibid., 'Anyone who browses through the advertising section of our illustrated newspapers today, will be forced to admit with amazement, that it was in advertising that poetry began.' Commodity lyricism 'harks back to those forms which were previously the preserve of literature.'

27 Also quoted from Genazino, 'Lyrik, wo niemand sie vermutet'.

28 Ibid.

29 'Bei Salamander ist seit Jahren der Wurm drin' (report of the general meeting), *Blick durch die Wirtschaft*, 6 October 1971, p. 5.

30 Genazino, 'Lyrik, wo niemand sie vermutet'.

31 Ibid.

32 Dieter Hülsmanns and Friedolin Reske (eds), *Aller Lüste Anfang. Das 7. Buch der Werbung* (Stierstadt im Taunus, 1971).

33 Friedrich Dürrenmatt, *Grieche sucht Griechin. Eine Prosako-mödie* (West Berlin: Ullstein, 1959). English edition *Once a Greek . . .*, trans. Richard and Clara Winston (London: Cape, 1966).

34 After a 'set-back caused partly by Bührle's trial for illegal arms exporting', the company's turnover increased suddenly by 25.4 per cent, thanks mainly to an above-average increase in the weapons trade from 817 million Swiss francs in 1969 to 1,024 thousand million in 1970 (This was due not least to a massive order from the Federal Republic's Armed Forces). The sector of turnover taken up by military commodities was declared to be 27 per cent in 1970 as against 21.6 per cent the previous year. However, it must be assumed that other sectors of turnover are devoted to producing materials used indirectly in wars. For the rest, there remains only a financial statement from Oerlikon–Bührle Holding AG of Zurich, 'which did not include the company's main area of business, the machine-tools factory, Oerlikon' (see 'Das Rüstungsgeschäft ist immer noch ein starker Pfeiler bei Bührle' *Blick durch die Wirtschaft*, 12 November 1971, p. 5.

35   Dürrenmatt, *Grieche sucht Griechin*, pp. 49–51.
36   These quotations are recorded in a curriculum report by Jochen Müller, in *Neue Sammlung*, 3 (1969), 217–21.
37   *Frankfurter Rundschau*, 17 May 1971.
38   Ibid.
39   If, however, a small shareholder should raise any objections at the annual general meeting, where he has the possibility and the right to do so formally, he may well be silenced with a blast of pop-music, as happened at the last AGM of the VEBA company.

> As the tumult of the shareholders' complaints against the executive board reached a crescendo, Birnbaum [the then chair of the board of directors] had to resort to a new weapon. Pop music suddenly let rip at full volume from all the loudspeakers, and where an opponent had been cursing and swearing, now only the song 'Moon over Naples' could be heard. After a few minutes the gesticulating shareholder, now robbed of access to the public address system, gave up. The participants sat down again and some even began to sway in time to the music. (*FAZ*, business section, 21 August 1971).

40   Benjamin, *Illuminations*, p. 243.
41   Ibid., p. 243 and note 21, p. 253.
42   Ibid., p. 243.
43   With reference to the bourgeois economists and philosophers, Marx explains in an aside this fusion of deception and self-deception; the deception being possible only through the self-deception of those who deceive the public. In volume II of *Capital*, Marx describes 'the label of a system of ideas', which is no different from the fully developed situation today, which we term its commodity-aesthetic appearance: 'The label of a system of ideas is distinguished from that of other articles, among other things, by the fact that it deceives not only the buyer, but often the seller as well. Quesnay himself, and his closest disciples, believed in their feudal signboard. [another early form of advertising] Our academic pedants do the same to this very day' (p. 435 f.)

Appendices

1 For a discussion of these and other problems, see W. F. Haug, *Warenästhetik. Beiträge zur Diskussion, Weiterentwicklung und Vermittlung ihrer Kritik* (Frankfurt: Suhrkamp 657, 1975).

2 *Öffentliche Meinung-Personalien-Neue Bücher*, 2nd ed. (Bonn–Bad Godesberg: Central Board of Advertisers, 1972).

3 Haug, *Warenästhetik, Sexualität und Herrschaft*.

4 T. Rexroth, *Warenästhetik-Produkte und Produzenten. Zur Kritik einer Theorie W. F. Haugs* (Kronberg: 1974).

5 *FAZ* 15 February 1975. Although in the clothing industry in the Federal Republic in 1974 altogether 60–70 leading manufacturers went out of business and more than 15,000 workers lost their jobs, nevertheless despite the fall-off in production of between 2.8 and 9.1 per cent, 'a new fashion input began an upturn in the last months of 1974.' A few days later the *FAZ* reported on the leather goods industry: 'This sector of industry considers fashion to be the ally of others' (19 February 1975). But in effect this means the following aesthetic innovation, for example: 'Fashion bags are now styled like a broadsheet with soft, rounded contours, clearly different from the sharp rectangle, typical of the earlier model' – which is now made aesthetically obsolete. In its leading article on the same day the *FAZ* informed its leaders that in the area of ski-wear 'all equipment older than 24 months will be written off as already completely out-dated' (19 February 1975). Similar announcements emanate from all producers of consumer goods. Obviously the economic crisis accelerates this process and the result was summed up some time ago by a market researcher at the 'Rhein-Main Marketing-Club':

Do we want our products to live for ever?', asked the pyschologist Wolfgang Wiencke . . . and he answered the question immediately himself – no. If in the life cycle of a production process or group of products, after introduction on the market, growth and maturing, a phase is reached when the market is glutted and decline sets in, it is at this stage that it is better to start up a new life cycle . . . The expertise of the market researcher underlines the warning to the company not to hang on to products . . . which are hovering on the edge of making a loss. From here onwards the projected life of any product, whether it be a cigarette or a car, reduces more and more. In ten years time 80% of the products on the market today will have disappeared. ('Die Lebensdauer von Produkten sinkt', *Blick durch die Wirtschaft*, 4 May 1974.)

To call this prediction 'the result of research' is not only an advertising joke but it also indicates the natural character of this process which acts as an 'external coercive force' for private capital.

6   *Süddeutsche Zeitung*, 12 October 1972.

7   W. F. Haug, *Vorlesungen zur Einführung ins 'Kapital'*, (Cologne: Pahl-Rugenstein Verlag, 1974, 3rd rev. ed., 1983).

8   All the questions of method that I have merely touched upon here are treated in depth in the *Vorlesungen*.

9   Vance Packard, *The Hidden Persuaders* (London: Longmans, Green, 1957).

10 Ibid., pp. 8–9.

Index